ENJOY SEX IN THE MIDDLE YEARS

Christine E. Sandford qualified as a doctor after training at the Royal Free Hospital School of Medicine for Women in London and was a general practitioner full time for nine years. She worked part time in mother and child clinics, and was a founder member of the Family Planning (contraceptive) clinic at Rugby. She still works in two local Family Planning clinics. In 1961 she became a Marriage Guidance counsellor and between 1966 and 1981 she was also a tutor in Marriage Guidance. She and her husband live in a Worcestershire village, where they enjoy gardening and rearing Jacob's sheep. They have three married sons and four grandchildren.

POSITIVE HEALTH GUIDE

ENJOY SEX
IN THE
MIDDLE YEARS

Dr Christine E. Sandford

Published in association with
the National Marriage Guidance Council

MARTIN DUNITZ

To my dear husband,
John Lindsay Banting

© Christine E. Sandford 1983

First published in the United Kingdom in 1983
by Martin Dunitz Limited, London

The names and circumstances of the people mentioned in the
case histories in this book have been changed to protect
their privacy.

British Library Cataloguing in Publication Data
Sandford, Christine E.
   Enjoy sex in the middle years.—(Positive
   health guide)
   1. Sex
   I Title.   II. Series
   306.7   HQ21

ISBN 0–906348–46–3
ISBN 0–906348–45–5 Pbk

Phototypeset in Garamond by Input Typesetting Ltd, London

Printed in Singapore by Koon Wah Printing Pte Ltd

CONTENTS

INTRODUCTION: THE SCOPE OF THE PROBLEM

Many couples go through the whole of their lives together giving and receiving pleasure from sex and gaining from it a sense of being loved and valued. The majority are content with their own kind of love-making and for them sex is not and will not be a problem.

Some couples, however, do run into difficulties with sex. Sometimes the difficulties are so great that they will seriously upset their relationship and even lead to a break-down of the marriage. Such difficulties are all the more painful when they occur in middle age – just at the time when people often look forward to a period of stability and happiness together.

The need to talk it over

My experience with the anxieties and difficulties people have with sex comes from a variety of sources. When I was a family doctor I often found that both men and women would confide reluctantly that all was not well with their marriage, especially on the sexual side. Later, as a marriage counsellor, I realized that the underlying problem as to why couples felt that they had run into difficulties was often disagreement over sex. Even if this were not the immediate reason the relationship had gone awry, other difficulties often affected the way they felt about sex between them.

For over twenty years I have worked in family planning (contraceptive) clinics and within that field I have more recently specialized in offering help to those with acknowledged sexual problems. About one-third of those who have come to seek this specific help have been in the age group of forty to sixty, that is to say, in the middle years. But for every one who has actually talked openly about a sexual problem, there have been dozens who have brought tentative questions and nagging anxieties that often point to an underlying sexual difficulty. They have found that as they have arrived at middle age there have been slight changes in themselves and their partners which are reflected in their sex life, so they want to ask questions and gain reassurance.

It is often because people have been coming to the clinic for some years for family planning and know all of us who work there well that they have confidence enough to tell us their anxieties, and though most of them are women, they will tell us of their partner's problems and often we have encouraged couples to come to the clinic together to talk things over. Regular attendance at such a clinic means that you don't have to have the excuse of some illness before you can talk to anyone. There must be a great many people, men as well as women, who don't have this opportunity.

Research and practicalities

Until comparatively recently, very little serious research work had been done on sexual difficulties. Then in 1966 Masters and Johnson brought out their book, *Human Sexual Response*, followed in 1970 by *Human Sexual Inadequacy* (both published by Little, Brown, Boston, Mass.) which were real landmarks in the subject of human sexuality. Since then a great deal of further work has been done both in the United States and in Great Britain and far more help is available to those in difficulty.

You may be one of the many people who still find it very difficult to speak about sexual matters, or indeed may not know to whom to go if you want to speak about such things. Interestingly, doctors and counsellors find that most problems they have to deal with in this field do not come from any real deep-seated ailment, but from a lack of knowledge, which then leads to anxiety. Your anxiety may well increase and make things worse because you find it difficult even to talk things over with friends and you are not sure who else to go to. You may find it deeply embarrassing and think that a doctor or nurse might laugh at you.

There are, of course, many books that explain sexual facts, especially since the work of Masters and Johnson, but most of them seem to be designed particularly for young people – certainly some of the illustrations, pleasing though they may be, seem to indicate that sex is the prerogative of the young, the slim and the beautiful. As well as those designed for the young, there are specialist books for the over-sixties and also for the disabled. For some time the National Marriage Guidance Council have been aware of the huge demand for a book designed to explore the needs of those in the middle years, and it is precisely to fill that gap that this book has been written. Among the people it is designed to help will be those of you who will probably have had considerable sexual experience, probably also growing-up families of your own, but whatever your circumstances, you will not feel that you are yet elderly.

Many people at this stage in their lives feel that they ought at their age to know all about this important physical and emotional area, or that others will expect them to have more knowledge than they have. It only increases their shyness when problems arise in their sex lives, especially when they're not sure who is the best person to turn to. I'm sure you would not feel embarrassed talking to your family doctor about your indigestion or a headache, whereas you might be very embarrassed at discussing a lack of sexual feelings or the occasional failure of erection. You might feel that he would think you were rather stupid, or even be embarrassed himself. Another thing – would it all be confidential? Would it not be seen as disloyalty to your partner? (Although these fears are not normally justified, they certainly make people wary of asking for help.)

There are of course other special pressures on you as you enter your middle years: children growing up and asking awkward questions; parents growing older and demanding more attention; pressure of work and of providing for your family and your old age, and the other uncertainties of the rat race – all these, while contributing to the depth and quality of life, create a certain amount of emotional and psychological strain. If to these you add changes in or uncertainties about your sex life, you can become very worried and unsure about yourself. Your sense of your own value as a human being may even be undermined.

In this book I will be looking at the following main areas:

1. Changes in sexuality and in patterns of sexual activity that occur in middle age.
2. Common questions and anxieties.
3. Physical changes in the middle years, their possible consequences, and what can be done to help.
4. Some common physical sex problems – known by specialists as sexual dysfunctions – and their treatment.
5. Contraception in middle age.
6. Sex in the middle years for those who live alone.
7. Where to seek help.

I hope this book will provide some help to those of you who have not been able to seek counselling yourselves, and that it will also prove a back-up to those of you already being counselled.

Above all, I hope that you will begin to realize that you are not alone in having questions you want to ask, anxieties which trouble you, or actual difficulties. Once you feel that there are indeed many others who have worries about their sex life – just as there are many who have worries about their heart condition or their arthritis – then perhaps you will feel you can seek the advice and help that will dispel your fears or at least help you to cope with any changes that may have occurred so that you can carry on happily and confidently.

1 YOUR ATTITUDES AND FEELINGS ABOUT SEX

Togetherness

It may seem obvious to stress that sex is much more than the physical act itself. Yet many couples who cease to derive as much satisfaction from sex as they once used to think that there is something wrong with their love-making. The truth is that the fault usually lies in their relationship with each other. Quite simply, until relationships between a couple are on a reasonably acceptable level, sex will also probably be unsatisfactory. It is for this reason that I want to tackle attitudes and feelings, which are often at the root of problems in the middle years, before going on to the physical aspects of relationships.

Most active bodily functions are accompanied by feelings. You enjoy a meal, the taste, the smell, the actual biting and chewing as your digestive juices flow. The pleasure can be heightened by agreeable surroundings and good company. Some foods of course do not give pleasure – you may not like the texture of liver or the taste of pineapple and so you will try to avoid them if possible, eating them only when driven by politeness or sheer hunger. On the whole, however, though you may like company as you eat, your enjoyment or dislike is yours alone, and does not depend on anyone else.

A question of responding

Sexual activity is one of the few bodily functions that is usually carried on with the participation of another person. The pleasure and satisfaction you gain is, at least in part, derived from the active cooperation of your partner. Moreover, in heterosexual relationships (which is what this book is mainly concerned with) two different sets of physical organs with differing types of sensation are necessary to complete the total act of intercourse.

Some people who find that they cannot continue to gain full satisfaction with one partner are happy to try again with someone else. However, most people in the middle years who want help with sexual relationships have a continuing relationship with one partner that has somehow gone off course. It may be that it was never quite as good as one or other of you would have liked and you feel that something needs to be done before it deteriorates too much. Or it may be that the outlook of you or your partner has changed slightly, or you feel you want to change and this can upset the old balance. Perhaps some anxiety about yourself, or your family or the circumstances in which you find yourself seems to be affecting your sex life. Whatever it is, it will have caused a loss of satisfaction to one or other of you which will almost inevitably in the end affect the other.

We have, then, to realize that there are two people and two sets of needs and expectations. Two sets of feelings are involved. You may be dissatisfied with what is going on sexually between yourself and your partner but it may not always be obvious to him or her. In some cases one of you may even continue to pretend that all is well. It can be very upsetting when a wife says to her husband, 'I've never really enjoyed sex since the birth of our last baby.' Her husband may well say with some indignation, 'Why did you never tell me?' His anger will be a mixture of feeling let down and of guilt that he was not sensitive enough to his wife's feelings. Often people conceal their dissatisfaction from a mistaken sense of loyalty to their partner or from an anxiety that there is something abnormal about themselves.

So let us look at some of the attitudes people have towards sex; but first we have to make a distinction between our attitude to sex, our sexuality and actual sexual activity.

Attitudes to sex

Throughout your life your own expectations and opinions will play their part in developing your attitude to sex.

These will include your ideas about what is right and wrong in sex and will be about other people as well as yourself. They will take account of the place of sex in the whole of your life, what you think about society's attitude, whether you approve of such things as titillating magazines or whether you refuse to look at suggestive TV shows. Your attitudes may stem from a number of philosophical, or religious, or sexist considerations but they will all have some bearing on the way you feel about sex.

Sexuality

Sexuality is not the same thing as sexual activity, though both are inter-dependent. Sexuality might be described as the feeling you have about yourself as a sexual being and the way you feel about others. Although femininity or masculinity come into it they are not the whole of it. Sexuality also has something to do with the way other people see you and this may not always match up to the way you see yourself. A clergyman once said to me, 'I'm often surprised at what women tell me about themselves and their problems. It's almost as if they felt that the dog-collar prevented me from being a man.' Indeed, there are many people besides ministers of religion who are often treated as if they were in no way sexual beings – the elderly and people who are handicapped to mention just two groups.

To be aware and confident in your sexuality obviously depends to a large extent on how happy and confident you are about yourself as a person. In other words, sexuality doesn't exist on its own, it is very much part of your whole personality. A lot of advertising, incidentally, is based on persuading us to heighten our femininity or masculinity – to boost our image of ourselves. A lot more makes use of feelings of insecurity, especially in the sexual field, and we are persuaded that all sorts of things from driving a particular kind of car to wearing the newest perfume, to drinking some special cocktail will enhance our sexuality.

Besides our perception of our total selves, including our sexuality, we also have sexual feelings related to different parts of our bodies. They can vary from the small thrill of having your hair stroked by a beloved hand to the overwhelming passion of orgasm. They can vary in different people; you may not like having your hair stroked! Some people scarcely seem aware of these feelings; some actually suppress them. This is an area we shall return to when we look at the physical make-up of sex in Chapter 2.

Sexual activity   This arises from the fact that human beings have sexual feelings. There are in fact both physical and emotional parts to this activity (see Chapter 3) though they are not always present at the same time. However, the really important aspect of sexual activity is that it usually involves just two people, a man and a woman. And in that simple sentence lies a large part of the problem.

Where a word is worth more than a gesture
When two people are involved in sexual activity we immediately have to take into account two sets of attitudes, expectations and needs. One of the complications is that because many people find it very difficult to talk to their partners about sexual matters, they may be unable to communicate their expectations and needs to each other. Moreover, how people see themselves may not be at all how their partners see them and vice-versa.

Barry, a forty-two-year-old taxi-driver, told me that he could not understand why his loving wife of many years had become cold towards him and then positively antagonistic; it wasn't until her anxiety finally drove her to seek help that it emerged that she had been brought up to feel that she must endure sex dutifully until she and her husband were forty – and that then all sexual feeling would die away in 'nice' people. Her husband's gifts of frilly nighties and perfume were seen simply as evidence of his depravity. Because she really loved him dearly she was very afraid that this 'depravity' might infect her! Since they found it all but impossible to discuss such things together, even these gestures, or signals, of his, so full of encouragement and caring, were misinterpreted. This so frequently seems to happen. Misunderstanding and distress can also arise when there has been an apparent change of signals. (In this context a 'signal' is a method of giving a message to someone by non-verbal means.)

During counselling, another husband, John, a post-office worker of forty-eight, said, 'I thought when she suggested going to bed early, that she meant she was ready for us to make love, and then she was angry with me and said that she was tired and that I never tried to understand what she felt.' To which his wife replied, 'That's all he ever thinks of. Doesn't he know what it's like looking after three teenagers – and he makes as much work himself.'

'But we used to go to bed early just to make love –'

'That's a long time ago. You were always the same – you just don't understand!'

But there had been a change and because they had never been able to talk together about sexual matters they had only been able to communicate by signals – going to bed early had meant a willingness to make love to both of them once, but now even those signals had changed. Now the same action by his wife no longer meant what it did originally and John felt he was being given false messages. In fact, this man did indeed care for his wife deeply, but because he had not understood what seemed to her a clear enough signal that she was tired, she made two assumptions: one that 'that was all he ever thought of' and the other that 'he doesn't understand'. Further barriers of misunderstanding were being built between them, and as long as they were not actually being put into words they simply accumulated and increased the bitterness and anger.

What influences your attitudes and expectations?

We all pick up ways of looking at things, from our parents and families, from our schools, from our friends, from what we read and hear. Gradually we build up our own code of behaviour, our own picture of how things are or should be and our expectations of how people are going to act and what they ought to do.

Family background and parental attitudes
These are perhaps some of the most important influences that develop your own view of sex.

Were you able to talk openly to your parents? Would they answer your questions truthfully? Was your natural curiosity about your own body and about the bodies of the other members of your family welcomed or were you given the impression that asking that sort of question was naughty or even disgusting?

Parents may themselves be embarrassed by their children's questions, which are so often asked loudly and seemingly always in the most public places! The easiest way to avoid answering is just to express disapproval of the whole subject. Sometimes parents hush children up and will only discuss such matters when no one else is around.

Older generations often felt that the whole subject of sex was taboo, so people grew up feeling that certain parts of their bodies and certain functions were nasty, embarrassing and secret. If parents – mothers in particular – had had unhappy or painful experiences of sexual intercourse, or perhaps painful menstrual periods, their own unhappy memories would only further emphasize the picture they handed on of sex as being unpleasant and shameful.

This is not universally true, of course. Some parents can discuss all bodily parts and functions openly and happily without necessarily upsetting a child's own inner sense of modesty.

Think of your own childhood, for instance. What category did your parents come into? Do you feel you learnt anything from both or either? Was sex something your mother discussed with the girls and your father with the boys? Could you compare your parents' attitude with anyone else's? For example, were your friends' parents more open or more restrained? Did you have classes in school where sex could be discussed freely?

Perhaps the most important thing to learn from thinking back to what attitudes we acquired from our upbringing is that there is no set standard of what is normal or acceptable or even right in sexual behaviour. Certainly asking questions is one way children learn and it is no more naughty for Johnny to ask why Mary hasn't got a willy like him, than it is for him to ask why she has blue eyes and he has brown.

If you feel embarrassed or shocked or disgusted by sex it will certainly affect the way you behave sexually with your partner. If he or she seems to differ greatly from you, it is certainly worth testing just how well-founded your own attitudes are. For example, you may have grown up believing that it is wrong to stimulate either your partner's penis or clitoris manually. Many think this is a natural part of sexual behaviour. This may well cause difficulty between you and your partner if he or she holds different views from yours. You should try to discuss this; perhaps talk about it to a counsellor and then reassess what is right for each and both of you.

Change
You may feel that the present so-called permissive society with its rising divorce rate, its sexual freedom for all ages and its explicit portrayal of

sexual acts of all kinds in print and on stage and television is more honest, more realistic and more sensible than previous generations. On the other hand you may feel that it has gone too far, thrown away too many rules and is indeed totally depraved.

Whether you take either view or one in between, you cannot be indifferent to what goes on in society around you. Some ideas may seem to you exciting and challenging, others repellent. Whatever your views, your partner may not agree with them. When your children are growing up and bringing in new points of view to the family forum there will be another range of ideas which you find you have to examine and make up your minds about.

I well remember one case, where currently fashionable ideas had a traumatic effect on two families. Two couples, Jim and Sally, and Roger and Belinda, were in their early forties. Both the men had successful careers in middle management, though not in the same firm. Jim and Sally had lived in their neighbourhood for some years and had three children of eighteen, sixteen and thirteen. Roger and Belinda had moved into a house just up the street four years previously and they had a girl of seventeen and a boy of thirteen. The two couples had met at the tennis club and had soon become very good friends. Their children got on well together, too, and happily waved their parents off to a weekend break which the four had planned at a big hotel on the south coast to celebrate Jim's birthday. On Saturday night after the dinner dance all four congregated in the sitting room of their suite upstairs. They were cheerful and relaxed. Roger looked at Sally and said, 'I really fancy you', and within minutes they were all laughing and discussing swapping partners. Although it was at first a joke, it soon became obvious that Roger and Sally were keen and Jim was soon won over. 'Don't be a spoil-sport,' they urged Belinda, 'it's only this once and we all know each other.' Belinda wasn't entirely happy, but she liked Jim, and Roger and Sally were evidently excited by the prospect. So they changed partners and went off to bed. 'I must have been mad,' Belinda told me later, 'but at the time it just seemed a bit of a prank and I knew that other couples had done it, and I just didn't want to be the odd one out.'

Of course, it didn't stop there. Sally and Roger found other opportunities, leaving the other two together. Jim and Belinda had intercourse once or twice, but often they simply spent the time together chatting as old friends. The day that Roger and Sally announced that they wanted to divorce the other two and marry each other was profoundly traumatic in every way possible and the anger and misery it caused to nine people's lives can well be imagined.

Counselling involved two, and at one point three, counsellors and took a very long time. In the end, seeing the devastation caused in both families, Belinda and Roger got together again and moved to another town, which involved Roger in a change of job. Jim and Sally remained behind, but their two older children left home as soon as they could. Picking up the pieces of their marriages was a long and painful process for all of them.

This is not the only case of swapping partners I have come across; almost invariably, the consequences have been out of all proportion to the idea of the evening's fun that the participants seemed to have expected. I doubt if any of those who took part would have done so if it hadn't been a bright idea that was around in society for quite a short time in the early to mid-seventies. Some of them, like Belinda, were very reluctant, but such was the pressure of society – 'Oh, everybody is doing it' – that somehow they got sucked in in spite of themselves.

Religion
However free-thinking you may be, you may retain some of the ideas picked up from your childhood. Others, who are believers, will see their sexual behaviour as being in the context of their relationship to God and to each other. This may affect a whole variety of subjects from contraception to the relative status of men and women in the family, to views on modesty or actual rules about what is permissible or not in sexual behaviour.

Cultural background In a world where there is a greater mobility of people within a country as well as between countries, cross-cultural marriages are increasing considerably. Again, each partner may bring different attitudes about sex into the relationship. These may not always be understood and can cause considerable pressure on both partners.

Overcoming negative attitudes

If a couple agrees perfectly on all sexual matters there is obviously nothing to worry about. If the partners can discuss differences openly and agree together on what they are happy about and what they can't accept, then again, there is no problem.

However, in the first flush of love people often give way more or less willingly to the one they love. A young woman will accept that the man she loves comes to a climax so fast that she often isn't ready herself, and will see it as a proof of his overwhelming desire for her. A man will take his newly-wed wife's inability to make any advances in love-making herself and to leave it all to him as evidence of her delightful modesty and as a tribute to his masculinity. After a while, both situations may cause resentment and give rise to difficulties between the couple, and in middle years these tensions often come to a head. In each case the way partners respond to each other and behave themselves may stem from deep-seated convictions about how men and women should behave.

So it is important to look at some negative attitudes that people develop, many of which are derived from the influences I have just been discussing.

In women
Here are those I hear most frequently from women who come for counselling:

'Sex is nasty.'
'Only men really need sex.'
'Nice women don't really have sexual thoughts and shouldn't enjoy sex.'
'Sexual intercourse should only take place for the procreation of children.'
'In any case, sexual feelings should fade out after forty – after that it's not necessary.'
'That's all men ever think of.'
'There are lots of dirty old men.'

Sometimes their husbands are included in this list of 'men', but sometimes they are shown as not part of this gallery of monsters, but again in a sexually negative way. Perhaps the most frequent phrase used is, 'He's very good; he doesn't bother me very often.' How sad to dismiss the whole joy and mutual satisfaction that can come from sex as 'bother'.

In men
Let us look at some negative attitudes I've encountered often in men who come for counselling:

'Sex isn't the sort of thing you talk about.'
'Sex is quite natural, isn't it, so why bother to talk about it?'
'Men have much stronger sexual urges than women.'
'I never have any problem with my sexual feelings and abilities. It's she that's abnormal.'
'Men need it more often than women.'
'It's a man's way of telling a woman he loves her.' (This usually of the wham, bang, turn over and go to sleep variety of sex!)
'It's manly not to show your feelings – all that lovey-dovey stuff is for women.'

Some of these statements may even make us laugh at the absurdity our rational selves see in them, but I wonder to how many of them you would answer, 'But that's true, isn't it?'

How do these attitudes particularly affect the middle years?

Again, I must emphasize that there is no set way in which people should view sex – nor as to how they should act, provided that each is content and fulfilled. Problems arise when one or both are not happy or satisfied.

Dissatisfaction   You may have accepted certain ways of love-making or intimate gestures of affection in the early stages of your relationship with your partner which gradually becomes less satisfying or even positively distasteful. Because you have never previously complained your partner may not understand or at first even recognize your dissatisfaction.

Change   You may actually change in some way. If you are a woman, you may be exhausted from coping with growing children, perhaps start going to bed earlier and resent being woken by your husband, however loving and ardent he may feel. Geoff is a man of fifty-four who manages his own business and has just started coming for counselling. He said to me the other day, 'All our married life I've been the one to decide on plans or initiate action. I come home tired and often feel almost too exhausted for sex. My wife seems to think I have stopped loving her. It's not so – but it would be lovely if sometimes she took the initiative sexually. I know that would give me a tremendous boost and I could certainly respond then.'

Apparent change in sexual behaviour, especially if not discussed, can be very disconcerting to the other partner and give rise to either totally or partially false impressions like, 'My husband doesn't love me', or 'My wife doesn't like sex at all'.

External circumstances   In your middle years, external circumstances can also alter the way you respond sexually.

Anne, a tired-looking woman of fifty-two when she first came to me, had an autocratic old mother in her late seventies, who came to live with her and her husband. The mother's bedroom was next to theirs and Anne felt that she must hear (and probably disapprove of) every squeak in their bed. As the relationship between mother-in-law and husband was already somewhat strained anyway, and the old lady was ruthlessly outspoken, Anne acting as a buffer between them, was on tenterhooks the whole time. It was not surprising that her response to her husband's sexual advances was not enthusiastic and she seldom got much pleasure herself. This led in turn to disagreements between the couple, the husband feeling that his wife no longer loved him and cared more for her mother's feelings than for his.

Age   You may be one of those people who expects your behaviour to change at certain milestones in your life. Sometimes a man can feel that at fifty he really does have one foot in the grave, and this is perhaps reinforced by the fact that his sons can now beat him at squash, or a younger man has got the job he was angling for. This may well make him feel that his sexual powers must be waning too! Anxiety sets in and, indeed, he may occasionally find erection difficult. He feels that his worst fears are confirmed and that fifty years spells the end of sexual activity for him.

Similarly, the menopause in women is another milestone. It is also one that is bedevilled by every kind of old wives' tale, often implying the end of sexual feelings. A woman may respond by saying to herself, 'Good, I shan't have to be sexy any longer', or by saying, 'Oh dear, I shan't be attractive any longer and my husband won't want me' – but in either case it will affect the way she behaves sexually. I shall deal with age and waning sexual powers (real or imaginary) in Chapter 6.

What can you do about negative attitudes?

Open discussion Try and discuss differences with your partner. Even if he or she finds it difficult to respond, it is worth trying to put your feelings into words in as gentle and loving way as you can, so that he or she can hear your explanation of what is going on.

Test the validity of your attitudes If you have deeply held attitudes that seem to differ from your partner's, try to look at them to see if they really are valid for you. Remember the taxi-driver Barry's wife earlier in this chapter who thought that nice women should have no sexual thoughts after forty? She told me she had been brought up, after her mother's death, by an elderly grandmother who was very strict and had herself been widowed when very young. As we talked, Barry's wife began to realize that she herself didn't really know why forty was the cut-off age and, although she had been quite ashamed of them up to now, she did have quite strong sexual feelings towards her husband.

I am delighted to say that this realization released her from her bondage to this old wives' tale. She was able to talk to her twenty-year-old daughter in a way she had never done before, she could let herself accept the frills and scents her husband offered her and have her hair done and dress in a younger and more attractive style. At last, and by degrees, she began to put her arms around her husband and to tell him she loved him. It transformed all of them, parents and children, into a really happy family.

Facts and opinions It is important to check on facts, and to differentiate them from opinions. It may be a deeply held opinion for many people that women don't have sexual feelings, but it is not a fact. There may be reasons for a man's constant need of masturbation, but it will not diminish his virility, or cause hair to grow on the palms of his hands, or make him bald. Find someone reliable to ask about these facts – perhaps a nurse or a

Discuss differences with your partner gently so that you can work through difficulties together.

doctor; or a family planning (planned parenthood or contraceptive) clinic is a good anonymous sort of place to go to. Don't rely on friends at work or the woman who has had every operation in the book. In later chapters I shall be giving many of the facts you need.

Prejudices   If something your partner does arouses feelings of hostility in you, do ask yourself 'Why?' Sometimes our prejudices can start from perfectly understandable events in our lives. One woman who complained that she thought her husband's obsession with breasts was disgusting, was able to recognize that her feeling of repugnance dated back to when in her early teens she had had painful glands in her armpit. The medical examination by a male doctor had involved examining and squeezing her breasts, which she had disliked intensely. This understanding enabled each of them to be more tolerant of the other and, by degrees, to free her from this prejudice.

Never impute motives   'My wife only lets me make love to her when she wants a new dress.' This can sour any relationship, but may be totally untrue. Sometimes insecurity can push you into seeing self-defeating motives which really do not exist. 'Nobody could love anyone as unattractive as me. My husband only makes love to me because he is doing his duty' or 'is sorry for me', or 'wants to keep me quiet' – or half a dozen other things that the poor man has probably never even thought of.

Be open to change   Even love-making can become rather stale and ordinary, even dull over the years. There is nothing exactly depraved in trying out a new position, neither does it necessarily mean that the position you have always used could never have been really good for your partner, nor that you will never use it again with pleasure. It is worth experimenting with new ways of making love like changes of position (see page 53), provided you can both be understanding with each other.

Loving and caring   Loving and caring are essential to working through difficulties together. Where two people care for each other, they will almost certainly overcome their difficulties. When caring does not exist no magic wand will put things right.

Giving to get

Loving and caring sometimes doesn't seem enough. This is the tragedy for some people. But a relationship in which both people are prepared to listen to each other, to do things for the sake of the other, to try and understand each other's needs as well as their own, this makes a solid base from which to go forward. The specialists in sexual problems Masters and Johnson call it 'giving to get'. It implies not that one person should sacrifice him or herself for the other but that the needs of both partners should be understood and met. You may have to spend time gently reviewing misunderstandings, you may have to be more frank with each other than you have been able to be before and in some cases you may have to face up to changes that you may shy away from at first. You are trying to be loving and caring for your partner, but it is just as important to be loving and caring for yourself. This way you can go forward together.

   In the next chapter I shall begin to look at the various stages in love-making, so that you can understand what is happening and how your loving and caring can make some parts of that process even better.

2 GETTING THE MOST FROM YOUR LOVE-MAKING

The human body can be used in many ways both to stimulate and to respond to a whole range of sexual activity. There are, in fact, so many ways of giving and receiving sexual pleasure that most couples should find something to satisfy them without offending the sensibilities of either.

Many people in middle age have learnt a lot about each other, but in my experience many can be helped to further increase their pleasure in each other by understanding the stages you go through in making love. This

There are so many simple ways of giving and receiving sexual pleasure.

will not only help you identify those parts not perhaps quite so satisfying as others, but will help you recognize that a balance of all parts is important if both of you are to get the most out of sex.

It is generally accepted by specialists that we have five stages of sexual response:

1. Sexual desire.
2. Excitement or arousal.
3. The plateau stage.
4. Orgasm.
5. Resolution – a resting phase as the body returns to the pre-arousal state.

I shall examine each stage in detail, explaining what each involves and why each is a necessary part of the whole sexual act if this is to be fully satisfactory.

Sexual desire, or libido

Most people know what turns them on and what is definitely a passion-killer, but comparatively little is known about why certain things provoke desire and others don't. People vary, too, in what sets them off – you may respond to a romantic atmosphere, others perhaps to aggression. Even violence and cruelty have been known to stimulate desire in some couples. In others it may be totally unacceptable and destroy all desire in one of the partners. Even if both enjoy it, it may have damaging consequences if it goes too far.

What turns people on?
Mostly, factors that induce sexual desire are quite simple and ordinary. Being together on a comfortable settee, warmth and cosiness, the curve of a breast, the smell of the body, will suddenly turn people on. The triggering sensation is often different for men and for women. Although it's a generalization that won't apply to everyone, sight seems to be important for men, touch for women. Certainly for many women tenderness and consideration are very important elements in the awakening of desire, and they find it difficult to understand that after a fierce quarrel some men want to make love there and then. A wife may feel that there is no consideration or tenderness in the way her husband has behaved and is still hurt and angry and quite out of the mood for love, while his passions have actually been aroused by her flashing eyes and flushed face. That is when she may well feel that his desire is 'just animal' or that she is 'being used'.

Fantasy plays a strong part in desire. We all have different imaginary situations that seem to excite us. Some people are able to share them with their partners and some can't. What excites men and what excites women is often different, too. Women can be scornful, sometimes disgusted by their menfolk looking at titillating magazines. On the other hand, women's magazines print hundreds of romantic stories every week which are bought by thousands of women. I wonder whether as they think over these stories they realize that the 'girlie' magazines are just as thrilling, but just as unreal and harmless to men as their own magazine stories. What they both do is make you feel good, lift you out of the humdrum, enable you to feel that you too are the golden, sun-tanned girl who has captured the heart of the dark-haired stranger or the handsome man of the world who can pick up any sex symbol he wants – just fun and no more.

This use of fantasy to see ourselves in imagination as a bit more glamorous than we really are can be very useful in helping sexual desire.

Contrary to what you might expect, couples that use fantasy actually find that it helps them enjoy sex better by enabling one partner to draw the other into the fantasy image, rather than reject him or her for not measuring up to it! Ageing is a mysterious phenomenon; few of us actually notice our partner ageing, and when you are in love, your partner can be

Ordinary things, like being together on a comfortable settee, may turn you on; tenderness is important for a woman.

just as glamorous to you as the fantasy image.

Setting is equally important and probably becomes more so in the middle years. You can put up with the back seat of a car or a cold bedroom where you snuggle together for warmth when you are young, but as you get older the comfort of a warm room, the pleasures of a bath, nice scents and soft light certainly set the mood.

Swings in libido   The measure of some women's desire is tied up with their menstrual cycle. Though this isn't true for all women, nor the pattern the same, many experience a drop in sexual feeling just before their periods, at much the same time as some have premenstrual tension. Often, too, they are not so interested in sex immediately after the birth of their babies – when, of course, their partners may well be wanting them badly, having perhaps cut down on sexual activity in the last months of pregnancy. The mood changes of the menopause can also affect desire and I will look at this in Chapter 6.

Men, too, can have swings in the strength of their desires. This may happen from time to time because of tiredness or worry, and can give rise to anxiety in their partners. 'Has he gone off me?' they ask. Provided panic doesn't set in, things are very likely to right themselves in due course.

Sexual attraction can occur between any two people and doesn't necessarily mean that you are on a slippery path. You can be attracted by someone who is not your partner and get quite a kick out of it, without ever wanting to take things further. To find other people attractive, even to let them know that you do so, can be part of the fun of meeting people. It need not be disloyal to your partner, provided that you know your own boundaries and make them clear to the person you are with, and that you recognize whether or not it is hurtful to your partner.

Arousal

For many people orgasm is the most and often the only important part of sexual intercourse. They find it difficult to understand that their partners may not feel the same or be able to reach that stage as quickly as they can. They may not even recognize that their partners are often unable even to achieve orgasm. It may be all that some people want, but it often leaves their partners high and dry and frustratingly unsatisfied. Moreover, it often has a cumulative effect. The man finds that his penis becomes erect and he makes an entry, and the whole process of thrusting and ejaculation is over in two or three minutes. As this becomes the pattern of their love-making, his wife becomes slower and slower in reaching orgasm and more and more unable to respond, sometimes never achieving orgasm at all. Alternatively, the woman who is able to reach her orgasmic stage easily is saying, 'Come on, get on with it', while the husband finds it more and more difficult to

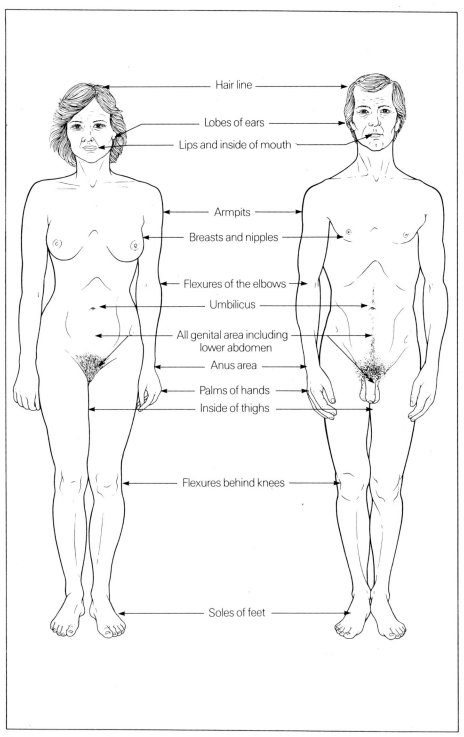

Hair line

Lobes of ears

Lips and inside of mouth

Armpits

Breasts and nipples

Flexures of the elbows

Umbilicus

All genital area including
lower abdomen

Anus area

Palms of hands

Inside of thighs

Flexures behind knees

Soles of feet

The erogenous zones are areas which are particularly sensitive in sexual arousal.

achieve an erection. For both partners to enjoy fully the orgasmic part of intercourse the preliminary stage of arousal is all-important.

By giving each part of the process of sexual intercourse its full value, you can gain something else too, especially as you get older. When one or other partner for some reason does not feel like full intercourse, either from tiredness, or illness or some other stress, there can be great mutual satisfaction in gentle and sensitive love-play.

Sensitive areas Apart from the sexual areas, there are special parts of your body which are particularly sensitive, the erogenous zones. These include lips and mouth, ears, nape of the neck, breasts, inside of the thighs and the area round the anus or back passage.

Love-play, the process of caressing and stimulating these sensitive areas, is indeed very like tuning up the instruments of an orchestra, until each one is responding on a perfect note and each part joins the others ready to burst into music. For this tuning process you can use your hands, fingers, mouth, lips and tongue. In fact you can use bodily contact of all sorts – legs, toes, the penis. This is in the arousal stage; later, of course, when the penis is in the vagina, the vaginal muscles also come into play.

How might you use these to arouse your partner? Well, you can tickle, caress, stroke, squeeze, hug, clasp, kiss, lick, suck, nip and bite gently – and a great many other things, for example, give butterfly kisses with your eyelashes! Love-play is indeed a light-hearted and happy part of love-making so often neglected by both men and women.

Again it seems often to be a lost art in the middle years. 'My husband can't be bothered any longer', 'My wife doesn't seem to respond and she never does it to me'. Yet how often the cry goes up, 'I'm sometimes too tired for intercourse, but I would just love a cuddle together.' For so many people it seems to be all or nothing, and yet as all parts of your bodily orchestra are tuned to concert pitch, it seems a great pity to lose the whole of the first movement. To continue the musical metaphor, many first movements can actually stand on their own.

The plateau stage

This is surely the slow movement. It is the stage when both partners move together towards the fireworks of the last movement – the orgasm. By now the preliminaries are over. Stimulation of other parts of the body will continue but the focus is increasingly on the genitals. Each partner has hopefully reached the peak of readiness, and should be able to signal this to the other. The penis slides into the vagina and the movements that lead up to orgasm begin.

Love-play is a light-hearted and happy part of love-making – don't neglect it.

This is a mutual stage where each can make sure that the other is ready and willing for orgasm. It can be a time of great closeness with each giving and receiving pleasure in a way that heightens it for both.

Orgasm

By contrast, this stage is a much more individual event. It is extremely difficult to describe, although it can be explained in scientific terms, which won't really give you the feeling. It has been called 'an explosion', 'the peak of ecstasy', 'letting go', 'going over the top', which gives you some idea of orgasm as a climax out of control – the moment you actually 'let go'. Although the other partner can heighten the excitement of orgasm, especially if the climax happens at the same time, it remains at the crucial moment an individual experience.

Out of phase

Simultaneous orgasms can occur, but many couples have individual orgasms separated by a greater or lesser time interval. It can be one of the changes in the middle years that gives rise to anxiety. Perhaps the interval becomes so long and one partner is so far past the peak that it becomes difficult to enable the other to reach that stage. A woman may find it an effort to continue the contracting and slackening off of her vaginal muscles, a man's penis may become flaccid and slide out of the vagina – and then the other partner is left high and dry. Unless the satisfied partner can take time and trouble to help, there can be a great feeling of frustration and lack of fulfilment left in the other.

This may well be yet another of the changes that can occur in the middle years. It can cause considerable distress, not least because the other partner sometimes seems oblivious of what is happening. It is perhaps more frequently husbands who are unaware that wives have not achieved orgasm. This is partly because a man's climax is signalled by ejaculation of semen (many women do not feel the actual event, but are aware of the extra moisture) and orgasm in the woman has no such obvious external signal. Besides, women frequently pretend that all is well and do not tell their husbands. It is often some time later, perhaps with bitterness and anger, that they inform their perturbed husbands that 'It hasn't been good for a long time'.

Physical aids

I want to mention very briefly here something about the aids to sexual enjoyment which may help couples. These aids vary from those intended to increase physical stimulation to those that work in the fantasy area. Some do both.

Vibrators Perhaps the most, and some say the only, important aid which is comparatively modern is the vibrator. It is a small electrical device which emits a very rapid throb which is used to stimulate either the clitoris or the inside of the vagina and so to help women achieve an orgasm. This may be an important factor in overcoming lack of interest in sex, or the inability in women to have an orgasm (see Chapter 8). Many women, however, use it simply as an alternative method of heightening sexual pleasure.

Sheaths (condoms) All sorts of sheaths are offered to men, brightly coloured, knobbed and ribbed, and with other additions. These are intended to stimulate sexual feelings in both partners, both by contributing to their fantasies and by physical contact. Whether they are considered frivolous or disgusting, the important point is that if both partners find that these aids do in fact help in the stages of love-making, then they serve a useful purpose.

Resolution

After orgasm there is a fairly rapid slackening-off period. The excitement dies down quickly and sexual organs get smaller and return to their unaroused state. Usually there is a feeling of relaxed contentment that often ends in sleep for both partners. Although some women can have multiple orgasms and indeed can go on to a further episode of intercourse fairly rapidly after the first, men, except at a very early age, can seldom manage this straight away. Increasing age makes a marked difference to how soon a man can have full erection and ejaculation again, and the same is true for orgasm in most women. Usually in men it is a matter of hours rather than days, but this can still make some men feel anxious.

Although people can and do have several episodes of intercourse at close intervals, on the whole couples have one at a time. I cannot emphasize too much that there is no absolute rule. It can vary from several in twenty-four hours to one a month or even fewer – if that is the way your body works, then that is perfectly 'normal' for you. Sometimes, and for obvious reasons, intercourse is more frequent at weekends or on holiday, or less frequent after an attack of flu or when you are decorating the house.

When things go wrong

You may feel that to compare the stages of sexual intercourse to an orchestra playing a symphony is rather far-fetched but the simile gives some idea of the way the whole body is brought into play in clear stages. However, to reinforce what I have said, in plain language, sexual intercourse consists of five parts, the desire to do it, a beginning, a middle, and an end and then a period of rest and going back to scratch. Each part has its rightful place and each helps to build up a complete and satisfying experience for both partners. If this is so, then both partners are content and happy with each other.

Change

It is when one partner is not satisfied with the way things are – 'making love isn't as good as it used to be' – that trouble begins and often this happens when the needs of one change. Change seems to be a word that comes up very frequently; we are curious creatures who get set into habits and often find change difficult to deal with even though we may realize that better things may come from it. We often feel too that the need to change implies a criticism of what went on before. It is this resistance that often makes those in the middle years not only slow to agree to change, but also resentful of the need to do so.

Sometimes, of course, this doesn't happen. Your dissatisfaction with sex may be only temporary, although it is possible that love-making will go on deteriorating and even seem to fade away altogether. Some people say, 'It's all right on vacation', or 'It's good if he's been away for a bit', but they look back to how it was and would like it to be better again.

What can you learn from the five stages to help to improve your sex life

See if there's a stage missing
If you look through the five stages for both yourself and your partner, you may be able to decide where your enjoyment seems to have faded out. Sometimes this is not clearcut. It seems to have crept up on you, or it hasn't been good for some time, but it's quite difficult to pin-point any definite moment. Again, what you can identify is which part faded first, and this can give you a clue.

Pain of one sort or another very often seems to be a contributory factor. A woman may have had a tear repaired after the birth of her baby; a man may have had a slipped disc which made movements painful. Whatever it was, it may have left a fear of pain recurring rather than pain itself.

Distaste can be another inhibiting factor. An unpleasant discharge which may have cleared up can still leave a feeling of revulsion. The very sight of a new self-lubricating sheath or condom (where the spermicidal jelly is already applied to the surface of the sheath and which can be sticky and messy) may somehow have set up a resistance.

Anxiety about all sorts of things can set off an unwillingness to have sex, or at any rate a tension that prevents the real enjoyment of it. It may be about becoming pregnant again, or that the children will come into the bedroom while you are making love, or it may just be that you are worrying about redundancy or the mortgage going up.

Illness of any sort can set up a fear or anxiety, particularly, if you have been told to cut down on your activities. In cases of heart disease, for example, people may be told how much exercise to take and what to eat and to cut down on smoking and so on, but they may not be told much about sexual activity and may be too embarrassed to ask. The advice would probably be 'A little of what you fancy does you good' – but it really is better to pluck up courage and ask your doctor. In this way a lot of unnecessary anxiety can be avoided. I shall be discussing the effects of various illnesses on sex in the middle years more fully in Chapter 5.

Events in your life can have ripple effects.

Jane, a woman I have been counselling recently, couldn't think why she had started not to want sex. How long ago had it begun? About three years, she supposed. Had anything special happened three years ago? Well, her mother had died, her father had come to live with them, their eldest son had left home to get married – and so it went on. When I pointed out that this must have been a pretty traumatic time in her life, she replied that her husband had been very understanding and supportive and that they had worked out things together and talked them over and it seemed unfair on him now when he wanted to make love and she just wasn't interested. It didn't seem to occur to her that any one of these events alone could have had a numbing effect on her sexual urges.

Identify the 'turn-off' point

What Jane's story illustrates is what we might call the 'turn-off' point. It is often very difficult to identify and people indeed need help to think it out. What you are looking for is the precise moment in love-making when you or your partner seems to be 'turned-off', unable to move forward into further sexual response. As the point nearly always occurs at one of the five stages I have described, thinking about these will help you to isolate the moment more quickly; not that it will be easy, for it is also nearly always the result of a triggering event which may have been forgotten or been lost to consciousness. Once the turn-off point has been discovered you can ask yourselves why this happens and identify the trigger mechanism. If both partners help in the process of relearning, the affected partner can be released and be enabled to respond more positively. Pain is a very obvious trigger. If pain occurs at the same time as sexual advances, then understandably the hurt partner will draw back from sex. But even when pain no longer occurs, the body may continue to draw back though there is no longer anything to fear. To recognize that pain no longer exists, to accept that negative responses are no longer necessary, and to relearn positive and pleasurable responses can be a slow and difficult process, for the fear of pain can sometimes cause as much distress as pain itself.

Bereavement is another common negative stimulus that can be as powerful as pain (see also page 31). Your partner may offer you the comfort of intercourse, but you feel it is not appropriate. 'I can't respond when mother died only two days ago.' It's almost as if sexual activity would show lack of respect to your mother, particularly if she was strict and disapproved of sex. The grief that follows death can have in it an element of guilt. 'I never really understood her – I often did things she didn't like – I haven't really been a very good son or daughter' – and so you somehow try to compensate by avoiding the things she would have disapproved of. Unfortunately, long after you seem to have come to terms with your loss, the negative response may linger on in sex and it can be quite difficult either to recognize it or to realize that it is no longer the correct one.

Coping with hidden negative feelings

Another negative response can be triggered as a result of sex being used as a hidden reward or punishment. Although it sometimes happens that sexual favours are given or withheld in exchange for concessions or promises, this isn't exactly what I mean. Those are fairly obvious attitudes which can be seen to affect sexual response. I mean something which is much less conscious.

You may be terribly shocked to discover that your spouse has been having an affair with someone else. You feel angry, hurt, disgusted, soiled – and it puts you off responding in any way to your partner. The reason is obvious at first. Perhaps you then make things up and the third person fades from your lives – but the poison remains. All sorts of things can trigger the hurt off again – your wife enjoying a dance with another man, your husband staying late at the office. You may try desperately hard to conquer mistrust, jealousy, fear and it is often hard to know where these end and where resentment creeps in. 'Why should I make it easy for him (or her) when he (or she) has hurt me so much?'

Gradually the conscious response may fade away, but a subconscious withdrawal may be caused by some quite trivial event, which even you do not notice. It is almost as if you are punishing your partner for the past, but it is also sadly preventing you from throwing off the past.

Getting to grips with the problem

Now, from your understanding of the different elements in sexual intercourse you will be able to:

1. Identify what part of the process is not working properly;

2. Think out why it has happened now or, if it has been coming on for some time, when it started;

3. Identify what happened at the start of things going wrong, and so to discover what actually triggered it off;

4. Decide if your 'turn-off' response to whatever acted as the trigger is any longer relevant;

5. Focus on any unaccountably negative sexual responses and see if they are at all connected with feelings you are trying hard to suppress. It is much better to bring out your jealousy and say, 'I know I now have no reason to feel jealous, and what a silly thing it was that made me feel jealous – but yes, that is exactly what I did and do feel.' Better to acknowledge the fact, recognize what it was that set you off and be more prepared the next time.

None of these things is easy to do. Even if you can identify them all, you may be left with the feeling 'How do I change?', 'How do I get back to where I was, or where I want to be?' This exercise does, however, enable you to understand several things: you can often see that you are functioning quite well in most areas and that only one is really affected. You can begin to understand what set the problem off in the first place and why your reactions, which were appropriate then, are no longer necessarily so now. Perhaps you can begin to explain more to your partner and enlist his or her help.

You will begin to admit to yourself that you have negative feelings even though you may not like them much. Then you can stop blaming yourself and start honestly accepting that you are as you are but that you want to do something about it.

You will begin to take responsibility for your own sexual feelings, and to decide what you want to do about them. This is really a very important step. So many people feel that if only – 'If only my husband were more considerate', 'If only my wife didn't always get so tired'. I'm not suggesting for one moment that you should insist on your rights, or demand attention, but rather that you should ask yourself the question, 'What am I doing to help my husband to be more considerate so that he can understand what I need and we can work together for better sexual relations?' or 'What am I doing to help my wife to know my needs and are we trying to work out together how she could be less tired, perhaps by changing our love-making to a time when she is not so exhausted?'

Sometimes you may both need some outside help to get through, even if you do begin to understand what has led to the problem, but often this kind of understanding, especially if as a result you can start talking to your partner, is all that is needed to set you back happily on an even keel.

3 HOW FAMILY LIFE CAN AFFECT SEX

Less time and space

One of the most noticeable things about growing older is that time appears to speed up! Perhaps it would be more accurate to say that time is taken up with all sorts of activities and responsibilities, and that you begin to find you have less time to fit in all the other things you would like to do.

Nowhere is this more apparent than in the time partners manage to spend alone together. Even if you do not have a family, social engagements, decorating the house, digging the garden, responsibilities within the community, greater responsibility in your job are all important and time-consuming activities. When there are growing children in the house, increasing amounts of time must be spent looking after all their needs and demands, and your own free time seems to vanish.

Having children at all will alter a couple's relationship, not only because they are the result of sexual activity together, but also because there are other persons to be considered besides the two of you; and those persons are demanding and time-consuming, however much they are loved and wanted. This is the situation in the earlier years and each family will set up its own pattern of adjustment.

Space – by which I mean somewhere where you can be alone with your partner – is also taken up. Many people encourage their children to feel that they can come into their parents' bedroom or the bathroom at any time – when the children are little, they like to wander in and climb into bed with their parents (they seem to like very early in the morning particularly). While this often gives rise to a happy, free, no-secrets atmosphere in the family, it does in fact make it difficult for a couple to find time and space for each other.

As your children get older their bed-times get later until they reach a point where they go to bed at the same time or even later than you do and even the peace of the living room is not left to the two of you. Once this has happened it can be quite difficult to change the pattern and tell children that you want to be alone together. Perhaps it is difficult to answer their inevitable 'why?'

Making time and space

Any relationship needs time spent on it and the space to be together alone, each giving attention and importance to the other. Nowhere is this more important than in the sexual field, and nowhere is it more often neglected. The children are safely deposited at the birthday party down the road. Do the parents say, 'Good, time to make love', or does she say, 'Thank goodness, now I can finish the ironing', and he, 'A quiet moment to fix the tap washers'?

Misunderstandings can easily grow when there seems no opportunity to be alone to discuss them quietly and slowly. You should not underestimate the importance of making this time and space for yourselves. You may be able to say, 'No, Dad and I are going for a drive on our own', or even to park the children with friends or grandparents so that you can get away – or even stay at home – on your own. It's certainly worth thinking about.

Adolescent children

The parents' middle years usually coincide with the adolescence of their children – a time of great change for the children, possibly even turbulence – and this can have quite disturbing effects upon parents, not least in their sexual attitudes.

Questions and challenges

The rebellious adolescent has become such a stereotype that we sometimes forget that teenagers don't spend all their time with chips on their shoulders. Even so, they can ask questions and challenge deeply held convictions, often in a very hurtful way.

'I shan't ever get married – it's so boring' may be a typical throw-away remark, but it does make you wonder what kind of image your marriage is projecting. Also, their light-hearted acceptance of a situation you consider should be treated more gravely, such as one of their friends having an abortion, may shock you and raise all sorts of questions in your mind about what you really believe is right.

Changes in society

We have to accept that society has changed. The oral contraceptive is readily available, divorce is not so difficult to obtain and seems to be more socially acceptable, abortions no longer carry the social stigma once attached to them, one-parent families are not only accepted but often given extra support. These changes in social attitudes, which seem to have come about so quickly and which are so widespread, will almost certainly be

Shared interests, which mean time and space to be alone together, help to strengthen and enrich a relationship.

36

reflected in your children's outlook and may well be in direct conflict with your own. Even though you may accept them in general, they can be very upsetting when your own family is involved.

Such changes may be very disturbing to you as parents and may make you stand back and look in an entirely fresh way at your own ideas about sex.

Struggle for power and divided loyalties
It can be particularly difficult when you and your partner do not entirely agree on what or how much change is acceptable. This can often lead to a kind of power struggle, where the young people try to get one parent to be their ally against the other. The pull of divided loyalties can be upsetting, particularly if you feel that your husband or wife is actually against you. Inevitably, this too can spill over into your sex life.

Jealousy
The other insidious peril that may be caused by your children is jealousy. 'She spoils our eldest son silly – I'm quite left out.' 'Oh, she's her Daddy's girl. I never get a look in.' Your pride and joy in your children can sometimes blind you to the fact that your partner may be feeling neglected and unwanted.

Envy
Sometimes you simply envy your children their sexual freedom, their apparent knowledge, the casual way they dismiss your cherished ideals, even the money they seem to have to spend on clothes or make-up or entertainment. It all seems so much easier for them and no one seems to disapprove or stop their experimenting.

Reassessment of ideas
You may be one of the many couples who do not find the new ideas and challenges that your children bring home threatening, and consider this part of your life together as very exciting. You might consider it a chance to rethink what you really believe, to test out new attitudes and to experiment. Often, in talking about your children together, you and your spouse can share reactions and be drawn closer together, sometimes by reinforcing what you both believe to be sound, sometimes in agreeing to change. All this can be very rewarding if it brings fresh impetus to your relationship – even if it is only the decision to spend more time together.

Children leaving home
As your children start to build sexual relationships of their own, you begin to see the change in their relationship with you, which may end in their forming their own partnership, their own family. You have all sorts of hopes and fears for them.

This is the time you start to question the way you brought them up. Have you prepared them for life? Do they know much about sex? Have you been able to talk to them? Do you know enough to help them, anyway? Should you tell them about the joys of sex or warn them about its pitfalls? Ought you to interfere in their friendships, or ask them about them, or leave well alone?

You may not even like their friends and be torn between saying so and pushing them into the arms of their boy or girl-friend or keeping quiet and giving them the impression that you approve.

When they finally leave to set up on their own, to get married, maybe to live with someone, this is again a new phase in your life. Each child leaves a gap, and the last to go a very big gap indeed. It can be a time of uncertainty and anxiety – but again, it can be a time of renewal in your relationship with your partner, a chance to recover and treasure the time and privacy you have together. A 'second honeymoon' is the term often used to describe this closeness and rediscovery of each other. With greater knowledge and understanding of each other's needs, it could be even better than the first.

Your own parents

Your own parents will by now be elderly and you may even have to face up to their deaths.

Naturally, ageing parents can be a cause of concern. They may not be able to do as much as they did before, they may become ill or infirm and you may worry either because they seem to need so much help or because they obstinately refuse all the help that is offered. If 'in-laws' have been a problem between a couple, their ageing is likely to make it worse.

The effect of bereavement
The death of parents will affect you deeply, whether you have been close to them or not (see page 13). Apart from the numbness which the event causes, all sorts of feelings of loss, pain, anger and guilt may arise, especially as you wonder whether you did enough for them, or could have been more understanding, or taken more account of their feelings and wishes. Often husband and wife can comfort each other, especially if you both loved the one who has died, and sexual intercourse may be one form of comfort. However, it is not at all uncommon for the partner who has lost a parent to lose all interest in sex for a time. It becomes a sort of period of natural abstinence – as if denying yourself the comfort of sex is an appropriate sign of mourning. Or it may be just that you revert for a period to being that child who is crying for mother or father, and won't be comforted by anyone else. Though this regression may occasionally tip over into a true depressive state, it is useful to understand that this is one of the normal

stages of bereavement which should pass in time. Usually, the depression starts two to three months after bereavement and lasts for two to three months. Partners need to be patient and understanding during this stage, but if it drags on beyond, say, six months, it is wise to seek professional help.

Your own ageing

This will affect you in a variety of ways. 'Middle-aged' can sound very set and dull and your half century may well make you feel very old; it sounds much worse than fifty, anyway!

It would be foolish to pretend there are not some changes, but many of them are worse in imagination than in reality and, again, if they are looked at squarely and discussed with your partner, they can be coped with. I certainly dreaded my fiftieth birthday, only to discover that I didn't feel any different from before, and in the days that followed the relief was so great that, of course, I felt much younger!

I shall be looking at the whole process of ageing in Chapter 5, and giving practical suggestions on what you can do to counteract some of its results and maintain a good sex life. But first I want to consider the effects your professional and social life can have upon sex in the middle years.

4 HOW YOUR WORK AND FRIENDS AFFECT SEX IN THE MIDDLE YEARS

A number of the difficulties that arise in the course of family life and that have to be dealt with by couples have to be faced up to in your work and social life. There, too, your ability to cope will depend upon your responses to change; on your feelings of anxiety, questioning, self-evaluation and the evaluation of your partner, all of which arise from change, and these will have a spill-over effect on your sex life. The same honest and open discussion of these changes in needed. You will need the same reassurances of mutual concern and love, and the same seeking of sensible alternatives to

Both partners will have to develop sympathy and understanding when pressures of work take their toll of home life.

previous habits that can help both of you to come to a new flowering of your love-making together.

Pressures of work

As you climb the tree in your job there will be the inevitable added responsibilities. You may not work in an office, but in whatever job, the senior people are expected to know more, to have the experience to be asked for advice, to set a good example and above all to keep ahead of the young people who are pressing on behind them. This could well involve you in extra hours on the job, more meetings to attend, perhaps out of normal working hours, and more travelling. This means you will be away longer and more often and may have to socialize, an aspect which sounds more glamorous than it really is. All this can be demanding, tiring and often anxiety-creating work, and can easily take its toll of your home life.

As such a person's partner, you may come to resent this intrusion of work into home life, especially the social side in which you are not included. Even if you are sometimes asked to join in, you may not particularly enjoy it. In self-defence you may involve yourself more and more

There may be problems of adjustment when both partners work, but these can be talked out, and you can give mutual support and take pride in each other's achievements.

with your children's activities, or fill your time with other friends and other interests.

With the best will in the world and even with strenuous efforts on both your parts, you may have less time together, diverging interests and little chance to talk. Each may feel pushed out of the other's life and it requires a real appreciation of the situation and a determination to pull together to get through.

When both partners work

What I have said in the previous paragraph will of course have a double effect if both of you are in full-time work. Increasingly now women carry on with their careers or take up their work again after the children have left home, or even when they have started going to school. This may be necessary financially, but it can result in increased tension between husband and wife. Part-time jobs tend to have unsocial hours, some being chosen specifically because they begin after the husband comes home from work, so that he can look after the family while the wife goes out.

If one partner is, or appears to be, more successful than the other, feelings of rivalry can arise and one or other partner may feel put down. As long as you understand that different people have different skills and abilities, and show proper interest in what your partner does, you can take a real pride in each other's achievement and give each other support when necessary.

Redundancy and unemployment

In a time of world recession, with less demand for goods and services, redundancies and unemployment are more common than ever before. They bring with them all the attendant feelings of being unwanted and useless. Curiously enough, we are having to face a new pressure: both partners find they have too much time together, the unemployed man feeling he has no real work to do in the home and that he is too much underfoot. If the wife continues in, or gains, a job of her own, the man will be left to run the house and family. This may add to his feelings of inadequacy, especially if he formerly left household affairs to his wife. She needs to understand this and to do all in her power to keep up his morale and to make him feel he is still of prime importance in the family. In turn, he will need to support her while the extra stress is put on her.

Retirement

Retirement and early retirement are both stages that require profound readjustments. Many people of course plan and look forward to a long and happy retirement with a whole lot of other interests which they will have the time to develop; some can only see retirement as the time of creeping old age and being on the scrap-heap. Partners can help each other by talking things over, by acknowledging their negative feelings and by thinking out ways in which they can make changes together. The comfort and closeness of sex at this time can do a great deal to reassure partners of each other's worth.

Repercussions

It is easy to see that if the pressures of work, redundancy and retirement put too great a strain upon the relationship at any one time, sex may suffer. Unfortunately, instead of saying, 'Our sex life is suffering *because* our relationship is under strain', many people think, 'There are all these difficulties *and* I'm not even any good at sex', thereby adding to their feeling of uselessness.

The affair

One of the hidden dangers waiting to surface at precisely this time when you are trying to cope with these extra pressures is that of a third person, who just happens to be close at hand. Whether friend or acquaintance, he or she seems to provide the sympathy and support needed at that juncture. This individual probably seems very attractive – and a great temptation as someone with whom to seek sexual comfort. If sex is successful with this person, it need hardly be said that other complications will arise, not the least being that if your partner finds out, the anger, jealousy and humiliation he or she feels is likely to damage your sex life. If the affair is unsuccessful, you are likely to lose self-esteem, as well as feel guilty and deceitful.

Why turn to someone else?

There are many reasons that can lead to one partner in a relationship having an affair with another man or another woman. Sometimes, as I have said, the other person will supply the understanding or the comfort or solace that one partner feels is being denied by the other.

Boredom could also lead to you seeking a new relationship. It hits most frequently at the partner of the 'workaholic': the man or woman who spends long hours preoccupied with work, often at weekends and holidays too; or the incessantly houseproud woman, who has little time for anything else, including her partner. A relationship needs cosseting. If you allow yours to become stale this will inevitably spill over into your sex life. Sex will become a dull routine and so affect even more the way you see your partner. It may lead to both of you seeking other people to interest and amuse you; at first there may be no thought of sex in such new friendships, but one thing can lead to another. Your new friend is almost bound to seem exciting and different when compared to your partner, and the attentions of someone who is younger or seems more glamorous than your partner can be very flattering.

Boredom can be the curse of any age but perhaps rather more so in middle life as relationships have had more time in which to mature or go stale. Don't slip into a life-style that excludes your partner, or leaves him or her alone for long periods. The dividing line between staidness and boredom in middle age may be a fine one, but you can, with care, keep yourself stable – and happy, and fulfilled.

Make the most of change
There is no reason why, however busy your life, you cannot be an interesting and exciting person. You should always find time to take care of your personal appearance, and you should try to cultivate interests that aren't entirely centred on work or domestic chores. Most importantly, though, you can deepen your relationship by showing interest and enthusiasm in what your partner enjoys. Openness to change and experiment in your sex life can be particularly helpful.

All these difficulties, even infidelity in one or both partners, can be worked through if both partners basically care for each other and are willing to make the effort. Change can be accepted and new approaches made, and this applies to sex as much as to anything else.

Recognizing that each stage of our lives brings differing pressures, which vary for different people, does not mean that everyone has inevitably to go through stages of trauma and unhappiness. Sorrows and joys are finely balanced to make life more interesting and rewarding and most couples make adjustments to both without too great a struggle. Sometimes you need to stand back and assess whether you have made these adjustments or whether you could do a little bit more to make the changes not only tolerable, but fresh and exciting too.

5 SEX CAN BE GOOD AS YOU GROW OLDER

It is fair to say that most people in their middle years don't like the change brought on by ageing, but the statement that 'your schooldays are the happiest days of your life' is really nonsense unless you have been remarkably unlucky. The process of change can be uncomfortable, but once we acknowledge that changes are occurring, and are inevitable, we can go on to understand what is happening and perhaps why, and so make adjustments both mentally and physically. When we have accepted the changes we will feel at ease again.

Let me give a very simple example. A ten-year-old girl will have no breasts to speak of and will not wear a bra. In her teens as her breasts enlarge she will probably need a light garment. When this same girl has her first baby and breast-feeds it, she will need a larger and firmer bra to support her milk-filled breasts and to make her more comfortable. In between her babies she may take a smaller size. Later, in middle age, she may need a larger size again and much firmer support with padded shoulder straps and elastic support to her waist. Although she may look at the little bits of ribbon and lace she sees in the shops with envy, she will feel much more comfortable and look better in a firm, long-line bra.

Being able to accept change in this way will actually make you feel more comfortable and happy about yourself.

Remember both partners are involved

Growing older together can be fun, but the ageing process itself can be upsetting to both of you. You may feel that the wearing of dentures, sagging breasts, an expanding waistline, or loss of hearing makes you unlovely and unlovable. It is probable that you are far more sensitive to these changes than your partner, who loves you for yourself. Sometimes refusing to accept change in yourself or disguising it – with heavily dyed hair, clothes a size too small and so on – may actually emphasize what you want to play down. In any case, your partner may not even be aware of the deficiencies that are so glaring to you. Your wife may feel that the grey hairs you so dislike are 'distinguished'; your husband that the middle-aged spread you try so hard to disguise enhances the feeling of comfort and warmth and security he has when you are around.

Your anxieties about your body and its functions could well spill over into sex, and inhibit you and consequently your partner. You can help each other in this situation. You have to be honest and realistic, of course – but you can also reassure one another of your love and appreciation. A husband might answer his wife's declaration that she thinks she ought to try and lose a few pounds with the remark, 'Yes, I think that would be sensible; you seem to have put on a bit after our vacation – but don't lose too much, I like you nice and cuddly.' This sort of remark is a real morale booster, both encouraging his wife to slim sensibly, but also reassuring her that he still loves her as she is.

The physical changes of ageing

You start to age from the moment you are born, but you don't worry about it until you begin to feel you are less able to do things than you were before. People are not always consistent about this; none of us seems to worry much because we lose the ability to suck our toes soon after we are babies (unless you're a contortionist, of course!). Because the years from forty to sixty are often the busiest of your life, you become aware that your body seems less able to cope with the pressures. Yet most of these pressures can be withstood satisfactorily if you compensate sensibly for the ageing process. Let us look at some of the commonest physical changes that occur:

1. Bones become at first more solid and then much later (from sixty onwards) more brittle.
2. Joints become less flexible and so do the ligaments and tendons around them.
3. Muscles slacken.
4. Fatty tissue seems either to increase – middle-aged spread is all too common in both men and women – or decrease: some thin people actually lose fat and become skinny.
5. Skin becomes less elastic, and more fragile; wrinkles form because of the loss of elasticity, and the skin becomes drier and more vulnerable to cracks and chapping.
6. Hair becomes thinner, drier and grey; often men become bald.

As these changes occur very gradually, you should be able to adjust to the differences in yourselves fairly easily. Nevertheless, it is sensible to acknowledge that they are occurring and devise ways of compensating for them rather than try to fight them.

What is their overall effect?

There are three main ways in which you are affected by these physical changes. Your body becomes less flexible and probably heavier, which leads to slowness and tiredness. You are more vulnerable to accidents, infections and degenerative changes, and often you 'just don't feel right'. This mood is generally a combination of a sluggish, heavy feeling and dissatisfaction with your overall appearance.

Changing your whole life-style

In this book I am looking specifically at how these changes will affect your sex life, and I will deal with that part in detail in the rest of this chapter. However, any measures that help you to compensate for the ageing processes will make you feel fitter and happier and this will in turn be reflected in the quality of sex.

Diet

What you eat is important. As you grow older you tend to need less food, but it must be the right kind of food. On the whole, the foods containing white refined flour and sugar are the ones to cut down on. Foods containing animal fat need to be taken in moderation because of their effect upon the heart and blood vessels. This leaves the proteins: lean white meat, fish, beans, eggs and so on are high on the list of necessary foods, as well as plenty of fresh vegetables and fruit, which provide many of the minerals and vitamins you need. Constipation is a problem to some people as they grow older and it is wise to include some dietary fibre or roughage in your diet.

Your appearance

This says a great deal about what you feel about yourself, but simply making an effort to look good and dress well can help you to have a good opinion of yourself.

I have two friends who both grew beards in their fifties. One grew his after he had been made redundant and the other after he had had a coronary thrombosis. In both cases this seemed to me to be a statement about still feeling able to adapt and move forward. You had only to see the way they responded to their friends' surprise and appreciation to know that they both enjoyed their new look and what it said about themselves.

Care of your face, hair and body, and dressing to enhance your personality doesn't have to cost much (though if you want it to, it can cost the earth). In terms of the way you feel about yourself and the pleasure you can give your partner it is well worth the effort.

Rest and exercise

A balance of rest and exercise keeps the body trim. I shall deal with rest later, under the heading of tiredness. Exercise is something many people in these days of mechanized transport neglect. I have friends who played tennis and squash well into their sixties, and are living on to an active eighty-plus, but this is the exception. There is no reason why these strenuous activities cannot be taken up in later life – indeed a reasonable degree of fitness can be achieved at any age – but it's important to remember not to overdo things at first.

There are many other less strenuous activities, however, which do not require so much physical effort and yet are extremely beneficial. Walking heads the list and nearly everyone can find pleasant surroundings in which to do it, even if it's only the local park. Perhaps at weekends you can get out to the wider open spaces, but even choosing to walk to and from the shops or part of the way to work rather than using a bus or car can help.

Swimming is another excellent form of exercise which, because water acts as a support for the body, can also be undertaken by people with stiff joints and aching muscles.

Bowls and golf are two more forms of exercise that enable you to use your muscles without having to move at speed and some people enjoy keep fit classes that are appropriate to their capabilities.

Exercise keeps the body trim and helps to maintain other activities, including sex.

Besides improving the flexibility of joints and muscles, exercise also helps to keep your figure trim and to maintain other bodily activity, including sex.

Keep your weight down
Here is a simple exercise to tone the muscles of your abdomen and help you with middle-aged sag. You can do this standing up and simply tightening hard on the muscles from waist to pelvis. Another useful way is to use the knee-elbow position. Kneel down and put your elbows and forearms on the ground in front of you; make yourself as comfortable as possible by moving the distance between your arms and your knees. You can actually comfortably read a book in this position unless you are very arthritic. Then tighten and relax the abdominal muscles as before.

These are general ways in which you can minimize the changes that occur as you move through middle age. I want now to look at some particular aspects in detail.

The knee-elbow position: make yourself comfortable and then tighten and relax your abdominal and pelvic muscles.

Relax and put your feet up. Short breaks during the day will refresh you and renew your vitality.

How to cope with the changes that may affect your love life

Overcoming tiredness   You may feel tired much more often than you used to as you reach the middle years. You end the day too exhausted for sex and you find it quite difficult to get to sleep. Rather than driving yourself on, it is better to devise short breaks for yourself during the day. Sit down for half an hour after lunch and put your feet up; collapse into that comfortable armchair and have a cup of tea before rushing out to mow the lawn. You may have to accept help occasionally or cut down on what you do.

Adapting to changes in your sleeping pattern
Changes in sleeping patterns may make one partner less responsive to sexual advances at certain times. The need for increased sleep or insomnia – both of which can occur in middle age – can have this effect. If you have tossed and turned all night and feel washed out and irritable you may be in no mood to join your partner, who has happily snored the night through, in love-making first thing next morning.

Talk things over with your partner, for apparent loss of interest in sex on either side may merely mean that the timing is wrong for one or the other.

Walking is a beneficial and not too strenuous form of exercise which you can do together.

Adjusting your pace

A general slowness, though not necessarily fatigue, is another factor that may be reflected in your sexual activity at this time of life. It may take a bit longer to walk to the shops, and it may take a bit longer to become sexually aroused. Since this may not be true for both partners you need to be aware of what is happening and perhaps adjust your own pace.

How to deal with stiffness

We are often quite tough with ourselves about our small aches and pains. 'It's only my silly knees,' we say as we painfully turn over in bed, or, 'Don't worry, it's only cramp.'

Stiffness and various aches and pains can make movement during sex more difficult. An arthritic hip may mean that turning is not easy. Cramp can occur quite suddenly and that can be inhibiting. Partners need to tell each other and perhaps devise positions which make things more comfortable.

Are you really comfortable in bed? Perhaps you need to look at your bed. Is it really still comfortable? Is it too narrow, or is the mattress bumpy or too soft or too hard? Do your bedclothes seem too heavy for you? Is it time to think about the warmth of an electric blanket? It seems absurd that people don't consider these things, but often sex can be a much more relaxed affair if you have enough room to move about and light, warm coverings. Sometimes extra pillows to prop up one partner can help to ease an aching back; and a pad underneath a stiff knee or in the small of the back may make all the difference.

Find the most comfortable position Sometimes you need to rethink the position you lie in when you are together. It may be that you can simply face each other, lying on a different side from before. Sometimes, where one has usually lain underneath and the other on top in intercourse, it may be more comfortable the other way around. If one of you has put on some weight, whether it be the man or the woman, the one underneath may feel squashed! You may like to vary positions, partly because this provides new ways of giving pleasure to each other, partly because rheumaticky aches and pains tend to move about.

It is difficult to say which position will be most comfortable for any particular couple, or indeed to say that any position is best for any specific disability. The sensible thing is to discover together what is uncomfortable and then to try out other positions, some of which you may not even have thought of.

For these you may sometimes even feel that your bed is not the best place. Some men with back trouble find that sitting comfortably in a fairly upright chair gives them support, and that their partners can straddle their thighs, supporting themselves in turn on the arms of the chair. This gives

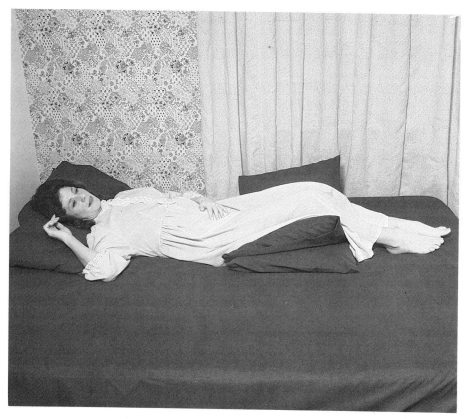
Find your most comfortable position. Extra pillows can help support stiff knees.

both partners a considerable measure of support which they can control.

Sometimes a duvet on a warm carpeted floor with several pillows that can be moved around will give couples space and a variety of positions to experiment with.

For many women kneeling bent forward, supporting themselves on their arms and elbows is very comfortable since it helps to support the spine and it is often suggested as a useful exercise after childbirth to allow the uterus to tip forward into the correct place, and as a position for exercising various muscles. Women can find their own most comfortable position by varying the distance between elbow and knee. Entry for the man is from behind. He can stand straddled, or kneel on the floor or on cushions, depending on his height and what is most comfortable for him. This position places no weight on the man at all. It lacks the closeness of a face to face embrace but it can be a comfortable position for both partners, with little weight bearing on either.

Tension and relaxation

The pace of life in middle age and the many pressures on you often make you tense, which shows not only in a restless mind but also in actual tightness of the muscles of the body. This can make it difficult for you to relax enough to enjoy sex.

There are some useful books giving exercises for relaxation like the book *Stress and Relaxation* in this series, by Jane Madders. Some simple measures that can help you both to relax are taking time to read or listen to music, or having a sauna or a massage. Again, a warm bath with a few drops of bath oil in it (see page 85 about varieties to avoid) or a shower followed by pleasantly scented talcum powder or body lotion can make men and women feel good. A warm room, shaded lights, and a comfortable bed with pillows to lean against can continue the relaxing process. Simply lying in bed, tightening up all over and then letting everything go can help muscles slacken off. One partner can gently massage the other at the tense spots – the neck and shoulders, the jawline, over the temples and the sides of the head, and anywhere else your partner indicates. You can use body or hand cream for this purpose and it can be part of gentle love-play which, where

An upright chair can give support to someone with back trouble. Your partner can straddle your legs with support from the arms of the chair.

Rear entry can provide a satisfying and comfortable position for both partners with no weight-bearing – some people find it excitingly new.

it takes account of the feelings of your partner without making too many demands or exerting too much pressure, is often one of the most acceptable ways of reducing tension in both of you.

Small ailments and how to compensate for them

There are many bothersome small complaints that can add discomfort to sexual activity as you move into the middle years. The ones that affect the genital area in women I shall be covering in Chapter 8. There are three other common problems that should be mentioned here.

The bladder
Your bladder can become more irritable and some older people have to get up at night to pass water. Intercourse can increase this need. Some women have a tendency to a mild inflammation of the bladder (cystitis) which makes it feel distended and causes not only frequent passing of water, but also a feeling of soreness. Cutting down late-night drinks, especially of tea or coffee, can help, and so too can avoiding acid foods such as plums or

spinach. If it becomes a real nuisance, ask your doctor about it. He may recommend pills if you have an infection, but he will also advise you about what to eat and drink.

Piles or haemorrhoids
These are swollen veins round the back passage, or anus, which can be painful at times, and the increased blood flow round the whole area during intercourse can make them more so, as can thrusting movements of the penis in the vagina. Ointments and pessaries and sleeping with the foot of the bed raised can keep them under control, but it is important to consult your doctor about them if they become really painful.

Discharges
If either of you has a discharge you should not hesitate to tell your doctor about it. Don't be worried if he suggests you go to one of the Special Clinics which have facilities to deal not only with VD but all forms of sexually transmitted diseases. This is probably the most satisfactory way of having your discharge treated. If you're very embarrassed, you can go straight to the clinic and be treated confidentially.

How illness can affect sex in middle age

As we get older, we are more prone to the illnesses caused by wear and tear and stress. The pressures I have written about in Chapter 4, combined with the ageing process, make it more likely that you will suffer from such things as heart disease and high blood pressure in your fifties and later.

Illnesses often have distressing side-effects and can make sexual activity between a couple difficult. You are not quite sure how often your sick partner could try harder or be less self-centred, and you often feel frustrated and cross – and then guilty about being so unsympathetic.

There is no doubt that ill people often have to spend so much energy on coping with their condition that they seem unaware of the effect upon those around them. Sometimes they make a great effort with people they don't know very well and little or no effort with their closest relatives, and in particular with their husband or wife. When they do understand what they are doing, they too can feel guilty but often quite unable to do much about it.

In the sexual field, because they are able to give less, they also find it difficult to ask for anything. This is the area where both of you need to talk freely with each other in order to reassure each other that you care still, and also to discover how you can give each other pleasure and satis- faction, perhaps in ways that differ from your previous pattern.

This may sometimes be difficult because what you are asked to do – perhaps what simply becomes evident as the only way to help – can be distasteful at first. You may be asked to kiss and to fondle the genital areas, mutual masturbation may have to replace intercourse, and so on. If you can both gently explore this new area of love-making then by degrees you will be able to help each other with love and understanding while respecting the fact that your partner may also be coping with considerable reservations.

Some common illnesses in the middle years

Heart disease
This is one of the increasing problems in the Western world. Lack of exercise, diets high in animal fat, putting on weight, smoking, drinking and stress are all factors that increase the likelihood of heart disease. Many of these causes are more likely to be present in middle age, such as stress or lack of exercise, while the cumulative effects of others, such as smoking, are also likely to appear at this time. The suggestions I made about diet, exercise and so on, on pages 48–50, are all useful preventive measures.

Experiencing a heart attack is frightening, and can leave you very anxious about yourself. Once you have been stabilized, however, you will be helped to come to terms with your limitations. Because, at first, you may be restricted as to diet, exercise and other activities, you may well be anxious about full sexual activity. Take your family doctor into your confidence and ask his advice. It is very seldom, once you have got back to ordinary life after convalescence, that full sexual activity cannot be resumed, but you may have to take things gently at first.

Your partner can help you gain confidence by caressing and fondling you and making you feel wanted even if, at first, you may not feel like anything very active.

High blood pressure
This is also a disease of middle to old age and its causes are very much the same as for heart disease. It affects about 20 per cent of the population, although many people don't know they have it. It is certainly wise to have your blood pressure checked at least once a year by your family doctor, as the condition is a major cause of heart attacks and strokes.

High blood pressure does not often have a direct effect upon sexual activity, but some of the pills prescribed may cause impotence (see page 79). Diuretics, which help eliminate fluids from your body, may have this effect, but not necessarily with everyone. They seem to cause the problem only in some men. Do tell your doctor at once if it should happen and he may be able to suggest an alternative drug.

Diabetes
This condition is also a possible cause of secondary impotence (see page

78). However, this side-effect is only likely to occur in those who have had severe diabetes for some time and have found it difficult to keep their blood sugar level under control. Only about a quarter of diabetics develop the disease before the age of fity, and about half develop it between fifty and sixty-five. Early diagnosis and treatment enables a diabetic to achieve control which can prevent the nerve damage which, among other things, causes failure of erection. Each person has to discover on an individual level what food, drugs, exercise and so on are right for him or her. This is an anxious time anyway, and the sufferer can feel pretty wretched until the disease and treatment are in balance.

Permanent impotence   If impotence is then found to be a permanent factor, you will have to discuss what you are both going to do about it. You will still be able to give each other pleasure in all the other ways except those achieved by erection. There are aids available (see page 60) that can enable penetration to take place without an erection; and you may be able to explore new ways of stimulating each other which can produce enjoyable reactions.

The most important thing is not to develop the attitude that all is finished for you sexually. It will come as no surprise that fear of loss of erection because you are diabetic is more likely to cause the condition than the diabetes itself. A few episodes of impotence do not mean that it is necessarily progressive, and control of your blood sugar will often reverse the condition.

Disablement

Disablement is a wide term, but here I mean a physical condition which impairs certain movements and activities. They can be subdivided into those caused by:

1. Injury, such as a broken leg or damaged hip.
2. Arthritis and similar conditions that are more likely to develop in the middle years when joints and muscles become less flexible.
3. Damage to the nervous system from injuries or diseases such as strokes, multiple sclerosis, poliomyelitis, and so on. It is very unusual for either poliomyelitis or strokes to occur in the middle years, but multiple sclerosis appears in a mild form at any time of life. Since it is a progressive disease, severe incapacity usually develops by degrees and this is often in the fifties, sometimes earlier.

Many movements can be recovered, even after massive strokes, but sometimes sufferers find it particularly difficult to achieve the specific movements which add to the pleasure of intercourse. In some diseases it isn't so much that movements can't be achieved, though that may be an additional problem, but that certain parts of the body can no longer feel anything.

These patches of loss of feeling are called areas of surface anaesthesia, and they are particularly likely to occur in progressive diseases of the nervous system such as multiple sclerosis. Sometimes they come and go, which makes sexual response even more difficult because the ability to respond to touch may vary from time to time.

Where to find help You will both have to explore methods of helping and giving pleasure to each other. In Britain there is an organization called Sexual Problems of the Disabled (SPOD), which produces literature on the subject and surgical aids that can support limbs and even, for example, splint a non-erectile penis enough to permit penetration. Your family doctor or the social services can put you in touch with SPOD. In other countries the counselling services listed at the end of this book can supply you with appropriate information.

Psychiatric illnesses

Illnesses under this heading are particularly difficult for both partners. If your partner is psychiatrically ill, he or she can feel very cut off and unloved and unvalued; you may feel that this isn't really the person you knew and loved before. You will feel alienated from each other, and won't know what to do to put the relationship right. Often even your support and reassurance will seem to spark off no response in your partner. If nothing you do or say seems to be the right thing, you may feel overburdened and lonely.

The feeling of being cut off from other people will often affect sexual relationships. The sick person will be unable to respond to sexual advances or to make any effort.

You will obviously seek help for your sick partner from your family doctor and possibly a psychiatrist, but it is often you, the well partner, who needs to be told what you can do to help. Talk to all those who are involved: your family doctor, the psychiatrist and the psychiatric social worker or nurse; they know that the patient's family carries a heavy burden and they will often be able to suggest ways in which you can help your partner when it comes to sex.

Anxiety and depression are mood changes or swings which can occur at any time of your life, but as responsibilities mount up in middle age you may not have the resilience of youth with which to overcome them.

Anxiety – the apprehension that something bad is going to happen – can simply be a highly charged nervous state, brought about by difficult circumstances, but which seems to have got a bit out of hand, or it can tip over into a real state of anxiety that needs medical treatment. Sex as much as anything else can be a cause of anxiety in middle age (see page 28). You or your partner could worry about the changes, real or imaginary, that

60

take place in your love-making: 'Am I taking too long to reach orgasm?' 'Does my penis become as erect as it used to?' Simply worrying about your sex life, as I have said many times, leads to less satisfactory performance and so a vicious circle is set up.

James came to see me because he and his wife had had no sexual inter-course for over six months. He told me that he seldom had any sexual urge and that when he did he found that after a very short time his erection would fade and he could not get to the stage of ejaculation. I asked him about what had happened in their marriage and he told me that his wife had had various illnesses, including heavy periods which had necessitated the removal of her womb (a hysterectomy), and that she now was being treated for high blood pressure. He talked of his wife with great affection, but I got a picture of someone who was frail and often in pain. She had, however, recently been talking wildly about ending the marriage because he no longer loved her. 'But I do love her,' he said. 'I can't bear to see her suffering.' I encouraged him to bring his wife the next week and I was quite surprised to see a well-built, fit-looking woman walk in. She was also angry. 'He can't love me if he never wants me.' He assured her that he did, but said he never knew when she felt fit enough. 'Good heavens,' she cried, 'just because I have high blood pressure doesn't mean I'm made of porcelain.' 'But your hysterectomy –' he said. 'That was years ago. You can't imagine that it worries me now.'

But it did; he had been so anxious about her illnesses and so riddled with guilt that somehow his sexual demands upon her had resulted in her heavy periods and subsequent hysterectomy that he had held back from sex for years until now he was beginning to be unable to maintain his erection. If only James had been able to share his anxieties openly with his wife or both had been able to talk to their family doctor, most of the friction between them could have been avoided.

Anxiety feeds upon itself, and one way to break the circle is to discuss the problem with your partner or seek help from your doctor. Certainly, as you read on, I hope that many of the fears you may have about yourself will be put in a better perspective.

Depression usually comes about after an unpleasant experience. Like anxiety, there are two kinds of depression. One is a real illness, where the depression seems to be out of proportion to the cause seen by the patient; in fact, it may just come out of the blue and there may seem to be no real reason for it. This kind of depression needs treatment by your doctor, who may advise you to see a specialist.

The other and more common kind of depression is caused by something getting you down. You may have recently lost a loved one, been made redundant, or become immobile through accident or illness. The depression can often follow a time of great activity when you have coped marvellously well. You may feel like bursting into tears; you may feel quite withdrawn from your family and friends; you may feel unable to make any effort to do anything, and you will probably not feel sexually aroused or arousable. Your partner's and your family's natural reaction to your mood might be to try to cheer you up or urge you to snap out of it. Unfortunately neither remedy works with depression.

Lots of misunderstandings can occur when one of you is depressed, partly because the depressed one seems unable to respond to understanding or kindness, or even irritation and actual anger.

Where medication can help Anxiety can be treated by your family doctor with tranquillizers and depression by antidepressant drugs. Usually the course prescribed will be short (unless you are suffering from the real illness I mentioned above), and designed simply to act as a prop while you steady down again. Some people, however, need the prop for a long time. Tranquillizers will calm you down, and though antidepressants are designed to do the reverse, both may make you feel rather flat for a time and you and your partner should be aware that this can affect your sexual responses.

How your partner can help This is where partners can really help each other. Talking together so that each of you can understand what is going on is all-important. It is better to allow the one who is really worried to discuss his or her anxieties in detail, rather than dismiss them with a quick reassurance that there is nothing to worry about. Gentle, undemanding love-making is ideal. This is another area where cuddling which doesn't necessarily lead to full intercourse can be very reassuring. The one who is depressed is assured of a comforting, understanding partner, who doesn't push further than can be managed and who accepts that temporarily nothing may be given in return. If you are not the one who usually makes the advances, this may be a difficult time, but try to offer your partner simple physical comfort and support.

Alcoholism
Much of what I have said about coping with pyschiatric illness applies to coping with alcoholism in your partner. One of the added difficulties here is that violence may erupt between partners and this may occur during sex. Not the least problem is the likelihood of impotence which can generate tremendous anger and bitterness between partners already at loggerheads.

Organizations like Alcoholics Anonymous and the parallel agencies that help families with alcoholics, for example Al-Anon, give information and support, including sexual help.

Don't let illness defeat you

Many of these illnesses develop or become more severe in late middle age, and some can affect your sexual activity. The first thing is to get the condition itself treated and stabilized as far as possible. Often sex will improve dramatically almost at once. Some drugs used in the treatment of specific illnesses can affect sexual response. If this happens to you, consult your doctor, who may be able to change the drug or suggest methods of dealing with such side-effects.

Sometimes you will have to be patient while your partner accustoms himself or herself to the change in life-style, and this may mean change for you, too. During this stage you may only be able to share limited love-making, but you can both enjoy this closeness and support.

Consult your family doctor and specialist about what is possible sexually and then take positive measures to explore what you can do. In Chapters 7 and 8, which deal with specific sexual difficulties that you might experience, I suggest what you can do to help each other. It can be a challenge but together, within certain limitations perhaps, you will find surprising scope and this brings a great sense of mutual achievement.

Gentle, undemanding love-making is a morale booster. When you don't feel up to full intercourse, cuddling can bring mutual reassurance and pleasure.

6 COPING WITH THE SEXUAL CHANGES

Over a span of about ten years in middle life physical sexual changes occur in both women and men. The most obvious change in women is the menopause – the change from being able to have babies to not being able to have them. In men it is a loss of physical strength and stamina with diminution of sexual performance.

The menopause or change of life

The menopause begins with a lessening of those chemical messengers, or hormones, in the blood that are associated with reproductive and sexual organs. This means that the ovaries stop producing egg cells and in turn the womb no longer sheds its lining during the monthly periods. The drying up of the reproductive hormones results in other changes in the body, and because this happens in a rather irregular way, different women are affected in different ways.

When does it start?
Timing varies markedly. Some women start the change in their early forties, a very few even earlier, but for most it starts perhaps in their late forties and is over by the age of fifty-one or two. Only very rarely do you hear of someone having a baby at fifty-five. On the whole, better health and better food seems to push the menopause into the fifties, but the timing sometimes runs in families. If your mother had her change in the early forties, so may you. The other factor is that the later your periods start in adolescence, the earlier the change seems to occur.

How long does it last?
There are, though, no hard and fast rules and even the complete process, signalled by less frequent periods and a lessening of their flow, and ending with no periods at all, may take just a couple of years in one woman or occur slowly over several years in another. The effect of the decrease in hormones continues for some time after the very last period until the body finally settles down to its own level.

The ebbing tide of the reproductive hormones, drifting backwards and forwards, not eddying here, now draining away there, produces a variety of symptoms, which gradually disappear, and a few changes which don't. I shall deal here with just the effects the menopause has upon a woman's sexual responses.

How you might feel about yourself as a result of the menopause

Many women have been conditioned to think of the change as an unpleasant time in their lives. There are two main fears. One is that you will 'have a bad time' with it. The second is that you will lose all your femininity, will no longer truly be a woman and that your attractiveness will go. You may find that you relate every little hiccup in your sex life to this imagined loss of womanhood, and this will only increase your lack of self-confidence.

Sensations of bodily change

Sensations of bodily change during the menopause often lead to a general feeling of being under the weather. This does seem to depend on how you respond mentally to the idea of the changes in your body and old wives are only too ready to shake their heads gloomily over the slightest headache or twinge and say, 'Ah, it's your age, you know.'

Nonsense! From childhood to old age we all get headaches and twinges now and again. There are sensible ways you can minimize the discomfort they cause, or you can make mountains out of molehills. Once you understand that hormonal changes do have side-effects, you can plan what to do about them without loading them with unnecessary importance. Sexually these feelings result in some lessening of desire.

The symptoms

The actual symptoms that occur can be very varied and you might have one or two of them, or all of them.

Hot flushes The symptoms that seem to cause the most discomfort are the hot flushes. They surge over the body at unpredictable moments causing redness of the skin and a hot sweaty feeling. They can last a moment or so, or several minutes and can be very uncomfortable and embarrassing.

Headaches can be severe but are more often only a sensation of heaviness and lethargy which slows you down.

Indigestion can occur, though again it is more often simply a bloated feeling in the abdomen, sometimes accompanied by loss of appetite.

Other physical symptoms can also occur: from tingling sensations in hands and feet, to dull and lifeless hair, to changes in skin texture (often affecting the kind of make-up you can use), and so on.

Apart from making you feel low, the main problem is that these symptoms make some women very anxious about themselves.

Mood swings are a disconcerting part of the change. You can be your normal self at one moment and the next moment for no apparent reason a feeling of gloom and despondency settles upon you which seems to have no connection with reality. You feel like bursting into tears for no reason at all and snapping at husband and children in a way that makes you hate yourself but which you find difficult to control.

All these things can have obvious repercussions upon your sex life. A feeling of being bloated and a hot flush just as you get into bed are not likely to make you feel like making love.

Permanent changes in your body

Those in the reproductive organs include, as I have already noted, the loss of the ovaries' ability to produce eggs, a diminishing of sexual hormones and the gradual dying away of the periods. It is the way that periods lessen that often causes the most bother. They can stop suddenly and never return for some lucky women. In others they gradually diminish in a steady way, with longer and longer gaps between until they too fail to return. The nuisance with these is that you can never quite judge when the final one has come, and this is reflected in sex, because you can become pregnant up to two years after the last period, since an occasional egg may still be released from the ovary though there may not be sufficient hormones to induce menstrual flow.

Yet other women have sudden heavy and sometimes painful periods followed by others in which the loss is slight, and this unpredictable mixture can be very trying.

There are good points too. Though many people are happily adjusted to whatever contraceptive they use, there is no doubt that one of the positive pleasures of the completion of the menopause is that you no longer have to be anxious about, or even have to plan for the possibility of pregnancy. Some people no doubt use no contraceptive and see the end of their fertile life as a great loss, but for most people the late forties and early fifties are not the time they would choose to have babies, and they look forward with thankfulness to the time when they can dispense with contraception.

A lingering fear of pregnancy can be a real difficulty in sex at this time, especially if the process goes on for rather a long time. Husbands may feel that by the time their wives are in their late forties they can't still be fertile and they may themselves be getting rather bored with contraception, particularly if they use either sheaths (condoms) or withdrawal as their method. They may become a little reluctant or careless, and this can put further pressure and anxiety on their partner and push her into avoiding sex when she can. I shall deal with the various methods of contraception suitable for the middle years in Chapter 9.

The vagina and outer genital region   Changes also occur in these areas. Some of them may sound a bit grim, but not everyone will suffer from them and even if you do have some of the symptoms they may not be severe – or even particularly noticeable.

The vagina is normally lubricated by a mucous secretion, which increases considerably on sexual stimulation. At the change of life this becomes less and in some cases seems to vanish almost completely; at the same time less fluid is produced and at a slower rate during intercourse. The result may well be that the vagina becomes dry and often quite sore, especially with the friction of penetration, and even more so if a sheath is used. A mild and bland lubricant is K–Y jelly, which can be bought at a pharmacy.

Another change is that the lining of the vagina shrinks and tightens and this, combined with the dryness, sometimes, though rarely, actually forms dry hard patches that can crack and bleed.

Meanwhile, the circular muscles in the wall of the vagina become slacker. Some women find that after childbirth another set of muscles in the floor of the pelvis which underlie the uterus never get back to their original taut position. They sag to a greater or lesser degree, and the pressure of the full bladder or the back passage can make bulges in the top end of the vagina. The common name for this is a prolapse, that from the bladder known as cystocele, from the back passage as a rectocele. Mild degrees of prolapse are reasonably common and not particularly uncomfortable or disabling. Bad prolapses are not only uncomfortable but interfere with sexual enjoyment. Sensation within the vagina may be lessened and since the muscles are so slack, they do not respond well to the effort to contract them. This considerably diminishes the stimulation which the woman can give to the penis, and so may affect not only the pleasure experienced, but may inhibit the man's efforts to ejaculate.

Other changes in a woman's external sexual organs include a shrinking of both the inner and outer lips that protect the opening to the vagina with a loss of moisture in their soft membranes, and a thinning and greying of the pubic hair.

Loss of breast tissue means that in thinner women breasts shrink and become almost flat, while in their plumper sisters, the breasts sag and become flabby with none of the taut roundness of youth.

Skin and hair are also affected by the menopause, though this is part of the general ageing process. Hair may become sometimes greasy and sometimes dry, but this changeable state settles down by degrees and in any case much can be done by way of general health care and judicious choice of shampoos and conditioners to counteract this.

What can you do to maintain a good sex life?

1. Don't be upset by all the negative stories told about the menopause. You may never have those experiences.

2. Do be ready to accept changes in yourself which may be temporarily uncomfortable. Knowing what may happen can alert you to the symptoms that arise and allay some of the anxieties about them.

3. Allow for the fact that you may need extra rest, a slightly different diet, and that your love life may therefore be adversely affected for a time.

4. Talk to your partner and your family. Reassure them of your love but explain how you feel. This may involve discussing changes in your previous pattern of love-making with your partner.

5. See your family doctor for the relief of minor symptoms. He may, for example, prescribe oestrogen pills or cream to counterbalance the sudden loss of these hormones in your body.

6. If symptoms persist, discuss with your family doctor the possibility of attending a menopausal clinic, if one exists in your neighbourhood.

7. In consultation with your partner, check that the contraceptives you are using are the best for you now (see Chapter 9).

8. Besides generally taking exercise in the form of walking, swimming, and so on (see page 49), try the following special exercises that can tone up the pelvic muscles and help prevent prolapse. Such exercises done regularly, though not excessively, will keep the muscles around and about the genital area in tone and can help considerably to enhance sexual responses.

Pelvic floor exercise
This tightens the muscles of the pelvic floor. Sit on an upright chair, with your legs apart. Imagine that you badly want to pass water, and tighten up all the muscles round the genital area as if to prevent passing water. Pull yourself upwards and inwards in this region to a slow count of four and then relax for a few moments before repeating the tightening process again. You can build up to doing this about twenty times. Try to do it several times a day. This is a simple and useful exercise and once you have learnt it you can also do it standing up, for example when you are washing up or ironing – or even standing in a bus queue.

Vaginal muscle exercise
This tightens the muscles round the vagina. It is best done in the bath, though you can also do it propped up comfortably in bed. The circular

muscles of the vagina only occur in the lower third of the passage, so you are concerned only with the lower 1–2 in (2–5 cm). Slip a finger – later two possibly – into the opening of the vagina to a distance of 1–2 in; tighten down on your fingers and then relax; repeat this about twenty times. Have a short rest and then repeat the process. You will find that besides tightening the walls of the vagina you will probably be doing the first exercise as well, but try to concentrate on the vaginal end especially.

Changes in men

There is nothing as obvious as the menopause in the sexual ageing process in men. They can continue to father children to a great age – Charlie Chaplin was father to his youngest child when he was 73. Of course, this implies that their wives are much younger than themselves. Nevertheless, the majority of men can produce fertile sperms for most of their lives.

There is great variability in how men change during the middle years, just as there is in women, and once you understand what is happening to you it will be easier to come to terms with the changes.

What men seem to notice more than women is their loss of physical strength and skill. This is particularly so in those who take part in sport,

Pelvic floor exercises help to maintain tone – see opposite for details.

for, of course, most sports depend not only on strength but on speed and co-ordination of hands, feet and eyes. Some develop a degree of cunning that makes up for loss of speed and mobility; others change their sport, but the day an active man sees he can no longer be really competitive in his chosen sport is a sad one for him.

What and where?

Tissues are affected in just the same way as they are for women. Bones, joints, muscles, hair and skin are changed slowly; more men than women go bald. There is a tendency to middle-aged spread.

Hormones There is no sudden cutting down of hormones in men, as there is in women. The male hormones, or androgens, do diminish slightly but slowly, and it is rarely compared to women that men need replacement therapy. However, the changing pattern of sexual response behaves in very much the same way of ebbing and flowing as it does in women; similarly, though some men notice slight changes in their forties, it is seldom that they are noticeable until over fifty and they are not marked till after sixty.

Less frequent desire It is often difficult to tell whether a less frequent feeling of desire is there of itself or because of the other pressures we have already spoken about which are part of middle age. You will often experience less urgency in your sexual feelings, though when they occur they can be as strong as ever.

Another element in the field of feelings is that there seems to be gradually less emphasis upon actual ejaculation. The positive side of this is that many older men derive great enjoyment from the plateau stage (see page 27), which they are able to stay with often for a much longer time, thereby increasing their own and their partner's pleasure.

Less rapid arousal By the late fifties it may take longer for a man's penis to become erect and it may require increased stimulation from his partner. Again this can be viewed both positively and negatively. The negative approach is to regard it as a failure of response; the positive is to accept it as simply a more gradual response and to focus upon and enjoy the sensations of leisurely and pleasurable stimulation.

Change in ejaculation There are various ways in which ejaculation changes. In your early years you may have had a slight flow of fluid that oozed from your penis before actual ejaculation. This may cease to occur with age. The process of ejaculation is experienced in younger men in two parts: a short period of intense awareness of the inevitability of ejaculation, followed by ejaculation itself. In older men the two stages merge into one. The force and the speed of ejaculation also change, and the rapidity of the squirt of seminal fluid diminishes by degrees.

More rapid loss of erection When ejaculation is over, the older man often finds that the loss of erection is faster than it used to be and in old age the penis may lose all its firmness almost immediately after orgasm. With advancing age there is often an increasing length of time before erection can occur again. As this often ties in with a greater length of time before a man feels sexy again, it often isn't noticed much. If you feel you no longer want sex every day or every other day, but perhaps only twice a week or less, then there is plenty of time for the penis to recover its ability to become erect.

Concern with your performance

A man's feeling about his virility seems to be closely linked to his competitiveness. I am not suggesting that women are not competitive; but rather that it seems to be a special element in the way men think about themselves. What frequently happens is that a man will have in his mind some standard by which he judges his performance. This concern with performance also occurs in sex and, of course, when a change develops, often a lessening of ability, it can be very worrying. 'Can I manage sex as often?' 'Is my erection lasting a shorter time than it used to?' If the anxiety is linked with other apparently diminishing powers, anxiety may become overpowering. You hear men talking about 'younger men catching up with me', though you seldom hear women talking in the same vein.

What can you do to maintain good sex?

Understand the slowing down process
If you know that slowing down is part of the ageing process, it will enable you to pace yourself and to realize that you are not losing your sexual ability completely. In fact, in certain situations, as in the plateau stage when older men do not feel the same urgency to ejaculate, it can actually allow you to enjoy this stage more and for longer.

Don't force yourself
Anxiety can often make you try harder and more often, if for example, you have felt that your erection wasn't 'good' enough. From what I have said about slowing down, you can see that this is about the least helpful thing you can do. It is really important here to understand that it is quality not quantity that counts. Having sex when you really feel like it, choosing the right moment for your partner and yourself, and feeling relaxed and happy about it will ensure that you can still have pleasure and satisfaction.

Talk things over with your partner
Your partner needs to understand what is happening too. She needs to be reassured that you are still attracted to her and want her. She may be as anxious as you might be at the longer time it takes you to be aroused. You might well have to persuade her to take a more active part for a change.

Take sensible health precautions
All the suggestions about rest, diet, and exercise that I spoke about in dealing with the menopause in women can usefully be applied to men, too. If you have particular worries, do consult your family doctor.

Explore measures for relaxation and toning up
Anxiety and external pressures of whatever sort increase tension in your body. A simple test is to relax your neck and shoulders *now*. You will often be surprised at how much they drop and how tight you held them.

Tension has an inhibiting effect upon most bodily activities, and sex is no exception. All athletes have to learn to use their muscles for a precise movement and avoid an unnecessary tightening of other muscles. Running, jogging, the correct way of playing a forehand drive at tennis, the swing

Anxiety and stress can increase muscular tension. Learn to recognize this and consciously relax the muscles involved.

Gentle massage is very relaxing and can be part of love-play.

of a golf club, all need a smoothly flowing action using the appropriate muscles, with the others relaxed.

Many of you will find it very difficult to relax and get rid of tension, but by now from what I have written you will realize that nearly all apparent 'failures' in sex can create the very anxiety and tension that can set up a vicious circle.

Each of you can think out ways of relaxing which are right for you. A sauna bath, a workout in a gym or just pottering about your garden may be your method of unwinding. There are some useful exercises in Jane Madders's *Stress and Relaxation* book in this series which you can do, or you can simply sit comfortably and work through all parts of your body, letting each one in turn go slack, tightening it up and slackening off again.

Massage is also very relaxing and here you and your partner can help each other. Gentle stroking and kneading of the 'tight' areas can be something you do for each other and may indeed be one of the preliminaries of love-play.

Exercise to strengthen the pelvic muscles can be helpful for men. The one I describe was first formulated by Dr Arnold Kegel, in the United

States, to increase sexual responsiveness.

The exercise consists of tightening the muscles of the buttocks and between the legs as if to prevent an urgent wish to pass water. Tighten and relax twenty times and then rest. This can be repeated several times a day. Don't rush into doing it too often or too quickly at first or you may simply overtire your muscles. Gradually build up the frequency. Later you can vary the exercise by tightening up, holding the tightness for a second or two and then relaxing.

Besides increasing blood-flow to the pelvic organs, this exercise focuses attention on the penis and the process of erection. This enables you to tone up the muscles in that region and some men find that they can develop more control over their erection. Once you have learnt how to do the exercise, you can practise several times a day, travelling in the car or train, or sitting at your desk. Don't expect any marked improvement, however, until several weeks have passed, when you will have gradually strengthened your pelvic muscles.

Can drugs help to compensate for the effect on sex of ageing?

You may have heard from time to time that there are drugs that can help sexual activity – that can increase your potency or make you feel more sexy.

Unfortunately, very few, if any, exist. Aphrodisiacs – substances that increase desire and potency – are still earnestly sought and many potions have been advertised with miraculous claims. If they appear to work, it is usually for three reasons:

1. They make you feel good.
2. They make you think you are enhancing your sexual powers, so you feel more secure and less anxious.
3. They damp down inhibitions in both you and your partner.

Alcohol, in moderate quantities, is a good example of a substance that affects you in those three ways – in larger quantities it actually inhibits sexual performance. But alcohol will not cure impotence (see page 77) or enable a totally non-orgasmic woman to have an orgasm (see page 92).

What about 'hard' drugs?
Just a few of the so-called 'hard' drugs are supposed to enhance sexual enjoyment, but their effects are so uncertain and often so bizarre that the experience can be more of a nightmare than a pleasure. In any case, hard drugs are so dangerous and have such appalling side-effects that they cannot be considered as suitable in any circumstances. Morphine derivatives and cocaine definitely impair sexual performance.

Hormone treatment

This is sometimes prescribed and can occasionally be of some use. I have already referred to the use of oestrogen in the menopause and though this doesn't actually increase sexual desire, it may well do much to make you feel better in yourself and, for example, make the lining of the vagina less sore, so that sexual activity becomes more acceptable.

Pills and injections (or shots) of male hormones are sometimes prescribed, particularly for impotence, but they are of only marginal use. There are comparatively few men, whatever their sexual ability, who are actually deficient in such hormones, and simply to give you extra doses of what you already have in sufficient quantity is unlikely to work except by providing encouragement.

Loving and caring

What I have tried to show in this and the previous chapters is that though sexual responses and behaviour may have to be modified as you grow older, they can still be the source of great enjoyment and happiness between you. A lot has to do with attitudes, your own and those of your partner and others about you. You can no doubt think of people in their thirties who seem to have sunk into an elderly mould and others of sixty and over who seem for ever young. I spoke in Chapter 1 about valuing each of the stages of love-making so that each could be fully appreciated. Perhaps the same things could be said about stages in life. You might always have enjoyed good food, though in your youth you might have chosen a hot-dog followed by ice-cream whereas now you would opt for a steak and a piece of Danish blue cheese. We do change and move from one stage to another, but we can also appreciate the good things about each stage.

I have described very simple and practical measures you can take to keep fit and to help you adapt to the slowing down process without losing your enjoyment of sex. However, sometimes you both need to talk things over and take stock. You need to look at whether you and your partner are happy with things as they are or whether you could adjust to each other to make sex more enjoyable for both. Above all, you need to avoid blaming each other for things which aren't quite right and to be open to change. That loving willingness to discuss, to accept, to act and to change might well bring you both through to one of the 'happiest times of your life'.

However well you manage to cope with the ageing process in the middle years, sometimes you are left with a failure of sexual function. Fortunately, these failures of function are few in number both for men and for women. I shall devote the following two chapters to them and to ways of easing them. They can, of course, cause a lot of unhappiness, but they can be aided.

7 HOW MEN CAN OVERCOME SEXUAL DIFFICULTIES

In this chapter and in Chapter 8 I shall be describing some of the specific problems that crop up in the sex lives of men and women. Although here I shall be dealing with men, general problems of timing, illness, drugs, stress and anxiety are, of course, common to both men and women.

Just as I hope women will read about those problems that affect men – and so be able to be more sympathetic and helpful when their partners are going through specific difficulties – so I hope, too, that the men will read about those difficulties that may affect their women partners. Sympathy and understanding based on knowledge will be an invaluable tool in helping your partner to recovery.

I have already suggested that during their relationship many couples may have occasional sexual difficulties and we have looked at some of the causes that arise during middle age. In some couples these difficulties appear to become worse until one or other or both of them can no longer enjoy sexual intercourse freely. It seems that an element of their sexual responsiveness is not working satisfactorily; in other words they now have what specialists term a sexual dysfunction.

There are in fact remarkably few types of specific sexual difficulty. Some are experienced by couples from the start of their relationship and some develop later. There are cases where couples have started their early sex lives with the problem, it has appeared to get better and has then become worse again in the middle years.

These dysfunctions are not illnesses in the normally accepted sense for they do not affect the rest of the body, except perhaps to cause frustration and depression, even anger. Moreover, each partner can often experience all the separate elements of desire, arousal and orgasm – but not when the couple are together. Let me give some examples. A man with premature ejaculation – 'He comes too fast' – has nothing wrong with the way his sexual organs work except that he cannot control how quickly he ejaculates. His wife may well be able to have an orgasm but cannot achieve it as quickly as he can, and therefore either does without or has to reach it by some other method. At this particular stage in their lives their timing doesn't synchronize.

There are illnesses and drugs that do affect sexual performance, either by causing physical damage of one sort or another to the sexual organs, or by acting on the nerves to these organs. They are very few and I shall be going into more detail about them later in the chapter.

It is clear that stress and anxiety are the most likely causes of sexual difficulty and that very seldom is the chemistry of the body to blame. A temporary upset in the working of the body can set off a sexual problem, but then fear takes over and makes things worse. This is both helpful and unhelpful. Unhelpful because there is no magic pill that will cure things, but helpful because it means that usually there is no underlying physical cause, so improving matters is often just a question of adjusting your attitudes and feelings.

Though I will list all the sexual dysfunctions it will be obvious that some people go into middle age with problems that have been with them for some time, even throughout their relationship. I want to focus on those that are more likely to occur, or possibly to recur, for reasons that are specifically related to the middle years.

Men can suffer from three types of sexual dysfunction:

1. Impotence or difficulty with erection.
2. Premature ejaculation.
3. Retarded ejaculation.

Impotence, or difficulty with erection

Impotence is rather a vague word which many men find alarming and shaming, and which is used very loosely to cover a lot of meanings. It would be more helpful to use the term 'difficulty with erection'. There are a great many variations on how this is experienced, but it is estimated that at least half the male population has had some sort of trouble with their erection at some point in their lives. From my counselling experience, I would put the number even higher. For most men the problem is shortlived and can easily be overcome. To look at this condition in more detail we must divide it into two kinds.

Primary impotence
The condition's name implies that the sufferer has never at any time been able to have an erection with a woman, although he may have been able to achieve one by masturbation. You can see that this is not likely to occur for the first time in middle age; it will have shown itself much earlier.

Of course, there may be some of you who have not had a relationship with a woman till later in life, only to find that you have this condition. Indeed, one of the reasons for the inability or unwillingness to form a close sexual relationship may well have been because of your anxiety about the sexual act, and you need to seek help.

Compared with secondary impotence it is very uncommon. Fewer than one in ten come for treatment compared with those who come with secondary impotence. If you include the occasional episodes of secondary impotence which most men have at some time in their lives, its incidence is considerably lower.

Primary impotence may well have more deep-seated emotional causes than secondary and be more difficult to treat. There is all the more reason for any of you who have anxieties about a first-time sexual relationship in the middle years to go and talk to your family doctor about it, for reassurance and help. If necessary he will recommend you see a specialist.

Secondary impotence

This type of difficulty with erection is very common, especially in the middle years, and shows itself in a variety of ways from a single incident after a heavy night's drinking to a total inability, apparently, to have an erection at any time. But the sufferer will at some time in his earlier life have been able to maintain an erection successfully.

Men vary enormously both in the degree of loss of erection and in their reaction to it. Some can have an erection which fades early on, some can get as far as wanting to penetrate the vagina only to find that their penis then becomes limp, others can manage penetration but find that their erection doesn't last long enough to ejaculate.

Timing and situation can also have an effect and some men can be potent with woman and not with another. Some men can also accept that this can be something which happens to them once in a while and not worry. To others a single failure can be a terrible trauma.

What are the other causes of secondary impotence?

Fatigue is sometimes the cause and this can be made worse if the man tries again and again on several days running, never giving himself a chance to recover from his tiredness. This is discussed more fully in Chapter 5.

Any illness that runs you down can lead to an occasional failure of erection. This can vary from the after-effects of flu to a chronic illness of long duration, such as rheumatoid arthritis (see Chapter 5).

Alcohol has already been mentioned as a cause, particularly heavy consumption of something like beer – and here a man may become more affected as he gets older or indeed when he is tired or under pressure.

Diabetes is sometimes the cause of impotence (see also page 58). Few diabetics are impotent and it usually only happens with developed and severe states of the disease. It is most likely to occur in those who have had the disease for twenty-five years or more, so it is obviously something which is more likely to appear in late middle to old age and even then only in those whose blood sugar has been difficult to keep under control. Rarely, impotence may be the first thing that shows in someone who doesn't know that he has diabetes.

Some drugs can cause impotence in a few men. Several types of sedatives, which act by damping down feelings and responses, can equally damp down the power of erection. Some drugs for high blood pressure can have the same effect. There are one or two other drugs that can occasionally produce the same side-effects, but they are rare and again can have different effects on different people. If you find that impotence is something that seems to be associated with taking a new drug do ask your family doctor about it. He or she may be able to change the drug to another that will help your ailment without affecting your ability to have an erection.

Pain can cause impotence. This is either pain connected with the penis because of injury or inflammation or something like low back pain – but this again is rare. Painful piles (haemorrhoids) can occasionally make erection painful (see page 57).

Rare causes   These range from such things as very large hernias to multiple sclerosis and some psychiatric illnesses may also affect the power of erection. These illnesses will be important enough for you to be receiving treatment for them anyway and you will be able to discuss problems of impotence with your doctor as well.

Attitudes to impotence are all-important   It is worth repeating that although I have listed several things that can cause secondary impotence, it is the reaction to the symptom in terms of stress, and feelings of humiliation, anxiety and depression that can change the occasional loss of erection into a chronic state. Even if the underlying cause is, say, diabetes, which is then treated, your continuing failure to have an erection is often more to do with anxiety about the fact than the disease itself.

The combination of any or all of the causes listed above with stress and anxiety can turn a few scattered incidents into a full-scale loss of the ability to have an erection, and, of course, every failure adds to the anxiety and inhibits you still further. It is a vicious circle, but one that you can break if you follow these guidelines.

What can you do about difficulties of erection?

1. Recognize that stress and anxiety are the prime causes   This alone can help you to stop worrying about failure of erection and give you a breathing space to take the following measures.

Don't be afraid of seeking help for sexual difficulties. A friendly consultation may ease a lot of anxiety.

2. Discuss the situation as freely as possible with your partner She may be worried that she is no longer attractive to you. She may even be worried that there is another woman in your life. The whole situation may be just as frustrating to her and because she doesn't understand what is happening she may not be able to help.

3. Have a realistic expectation of what is normal behaviour. Attitudes in modern life push you into believing that the average man should be sexually active very frequently and at the drop of a hat. Real life is not like this. Both men and women need time off and frequency of intercourse will vary, and sensibly so, with what is happening in the rest of their lives. Again, much unhappiness can be avoided if this is discussed between the partners.

4. Go and discuss things with your family doctor if the number of failures of erection doesn't seem to be explained by any obvious factor. It is sensible to take into account diabetes, for instance, or any drugs you are taking, for either would mean one less anxiety.

5. Don't be afraid of seeking further help, either by discussing the situation further with your own doctor or by being referred to someone who specializes in sexual difficulties. I give a list of other sources of help in the last chapter.

6. Look for contributory factors and deal with anything that might be putting an extra strain on you. This may mean cutting down on alcohol consumption, or getting your haemorrhoids (piles) dealt with. It may mean that you need a relaxing holiday, or just to take on less overtime temporarily.

7. Enjoy other aspects of sex Perhaps the most distressing part of impotence for both partners is the all-or-nothing situation. So often loving contact is prevented by the man thinking, 'I daren't start anything, because if I do I won't be able to have or maintain my erection.' And so partners can't even give each other the comfort of cuddling and caressing. It would be far better to say, 'Let's have a cuddle – I don't think I can do much more tonight.'

What your partner can do to help

Partners can be of tremendous help if they can understand what is going on and can be reassured that they are still loved.

Some wives can make it more difficult for their husbands by exerting conscious or, more especially, unconscious pressure, often through lack of understanding: 'What's the matter with you – have you got another woman?', 'You can't be tired all the time', 'You're a useless lover'.

Unconscious pressure can actually arise from caring too much. The wife who is unable to make any advances herself and reacts within herself by saying, 'I won't bother him', may make her husband feel even more rejected. The anxious woman who keeps imploring her man to go and see a doctor may have a lot of sense on her side, but her very desperation may increase his apprehension. Dealing with the situation sympathetically requires a nice blend of acceptance and reassurance and a calm discussion.

To the woman who is this man's partner, I would say that you can be the best tonic he can have if you treat his anxieties seriously without letting them become a major problem, and make him feel secure in your love without feeling that he has to achieve too much. This can be done with gentle, undemanding love-play.

Unfortunately there is no way of reversing secondary impotence immediately. Too many emotional and perhaps physical factors may be involved, but if you are prepared to take things slowly, most men can and are helped in my experience. A long-term condition is obviously more difficult than one of lesser duration, but confidence can be restored and in the process you may both learn to value and enjoy other parts of your sex life together.

Premature ejaculation

Premature ejaculation is another common sexual difficulty in which ejaculation follows rapidly after erection. In other words you may be able to control your erection, but once it has reached a certain point you have no control over your ejaculation. This may be before you can get near your partner, or before you can penetrate the vagina, or after only one or two thrusts within the vagina. It can be very frustrating for your partner, who has little or no time to be aroused, and, of course, it is for you too, both on account of your partner, and because the whole episode is so brief and out of your control.

It is usually a young man's complaint which may steady down as his relationship with his partner develops, but it may, without help, persist. It isn't often, therefore, that it is experienced for the first time in middle life. What does occasionally happen is that someone who has had it in younger days and more or less controlled it, may find that it recurs in middle age under conditions of fatigue or stress.

Rarely, it may be a side-effect of some illness, for example, multiple sclerosis. Fortunately, premature ejaculation is a condition which can be helped fairly readily. All the factors of fatigue, stress and anxiety have to be dealt with, and actual illnesses or drug reactions taken into account, but the treatment consists in helping sufferers to learn to exercise voluntary control over their ejaculation.

There are two main methods of helping you to do this. Both really need expert teaching and follow-up to ensure success so I will only describe them in general terms and encourage you to find out about details from a counsellor.

What to do about it

The stop-start method encourages you to have an erection, and to get towards feeling like having an ejaculation and then to stop the process voluntarily. Erection is then achieved again through stimulation of the penis either by you or by your partner, and again the process is stopped as you approach feeling like ejaculating. Gradually you will learn both to recognize and to control the arrival of this particular moment. Timing, pacing and frequency and several other details are important and special for each individual, so informed help is required for assessment, teaching and follow-up.

The squeeze technique is another method of helping you gain control. Your partner helps in this case by exerting gentle pressure on the penis with finger and thumb as you signal the approaching moment, and voluntary control is gradually established. Again, you need to be shown exactly how to do this, and where, if the method is to be fully effective.

Both methods usually have good and rapid results if you come for help fairly soon, especially in the case of a recurrence in middle age, when you have already established control once before.

If, however, you come for treatment only in middle age with a long-established condition that may even be getting worse, treatment is not so easy. Both you and your partner may have built up negative reactions which you may have to work through before you can begin to use either technique. For example, a woman whose husband consistently ejaculates before she is fully aroused, may never reach an orgasm by what she considers to be the right methods. Her frustration and anger at her husband may cause her to be antagonistic to her husband's demands. He, in turn, can feel rejected by her, but apparently powerless to prevent the speed of his coming to ejaculation; this feeling of failure may even lead to secondary impotence. Although the techniques may be successful in the end, both partners will need to work through their negative feelings first.

Retarded ejaculation

Retarded ejaculation is a comparatively unusual difficulty but it can be a very frustrating one. You can have a perfectly satisfactory erection and then find great difficulty in ejaculating. Some men can maintain an erection for a considerable length of time and still be unable to ejaculate; others can achieve only a trickle of seminal fluid from the penis; others again find that by degrees their erection diminishes as well and that secondary impotence may be added to the condition.

What can be done?
It is seldom that a man has had this condition throughout his life and in many cases he can still ejaculate if he masturbates. This suggests that there is an emotional reason behind this 'holding back' and the treatment is to discover what this is and encourage you to learn to let go, or give, again.

This condition needs to be clearly distinguished from the situation in middle to later life which I described in Chapter 6, where a man may simply not want to ejaculate every time he has intercourse. This, though more likely in men over sixty, can nevertheless be quite a common occurrence for some younger men, who enjoy love-play, erection and penetration but don't always want to continue to ejaculation. It is a very similar situation to one in women, who sometimes enjoy love-play but don't want to go on inevitably to full intercourse. This needs to be explained to your partner, but if both understand, are not anxious about it, and enjoy what you do together, it presents no problem.

Indeed, discussing things between yourselves is a point I make no apology for repeating. There is almost no problem you can't alleviate by talking it through.

8 HOW WOMEN CAN OVERCOME SEXUAL DIFFICULTIES

As I said in the last chapter, some special problems are common to both men and women and I looked at those of timing, illness, drugs, stress and anxiety. In this chapter I want to look at sexual problems specific to women. A particularly worrying problem, vaginismus (vaginal muscle spasm), I have included under painful sexual intercourse, which I shall deal with first. The other two problems are failure of orgasm and general lack of interest in sex – often inaccurately called frigidity.

Some of these special problems are more likely to be found in younger women, but it is important to differentiate between them and I shall give you an idea of how common they are in middle age under the separate headings.

Painful sexual intercourse

There are a number of causes of painful sexual intercourse, most of them fairly minor in themselves. However, there are some which are more severe and all can be made worse by fear of recurring pain. I am not including in the list general bodily conditions such as arthritis (for those see Chapter 5), but rather those that are confined to the genital areas. There is much that can be done to make intercourse less painful, and I have included advice on this in a section following the descriptions of conditions.

Conditions affecting the vagina

The hymen is the membrane which in children almost covers the opening to the vagina. Natural stretching, physical exercise and the use of tampons during the monthly periods are some of the reasons why the hymen nowadays seldom remains unstretched even before a woman's first experience of sexual intercourse. It is unlikely, therefore, to be a problem for women in middle age. However, very rarely, I have found a small remaining tag of hymen that occasionally gets caught during penetration. This can set up a sudden sharp pain which causes a tightening of the vaginal muscles in recoil and may lead to vaginismus (see page 86). A very simple little operation can remove the tag; but I must reiterate that this is not at all likely in middle age, except possibly for a woman who has never previously had sexual intercourse.

Cuts and splits and other physical damage can occur, usually at the opening of the vagina, from something quite simple, for example, catching the soft skin round the area with a finger-nail while washing or inserting a tampon. If tears occur during childbirth the resulting stitching can sometimes result in scar tissue which can itself be painful, or may be covered with such thin skin that it is very easily scratched. It is sensible to go to your family doctor for advice and treatment, rather than use the cream or lotion you usually put on cuts and abrasions on other parts of the body as the skin in the genital area is so sensitive.

Infections and discharges can also cause painful intercourse. Vaginal discharge, for instance, may occur only occasionally and be hardly noticeable. But it is important to let your family doctor have a look at it, especially if it becomes more profuse and irritating. This can certainly make intercourse very uncomfortable and even painful. It can be caused by a variety of organisms; perhaps the commonest is thrush, or *Trichomonas vaginalis*. This can affect men as well, but seldom in a noticeable way. What happens is that without being aware of it, they may harbour the organisms within the penis, and even if wives are successfully treated, they can be reinfected from their husbands. So it is important that both partners are treated together to ensure that they don't pass it backwards and forwards. Treatment normally consists of a course of pills, backed up by vaginal pessaries and sometimes cream to use on the penis.

Often we carry minor organisms on our bodies, where they exist in small colonies that do no harm; but if the right conditions occur they multiply rapidly. The vagina can provide just such conditions, so take some simple precautions to lessen the likelihood of it being a breeding ground for harmful organisms.

- Don't wear synthetic fibres next to the genital area: they often exclude the free passage of air. Many women wear tights, nylon pants and even trousers, one on top of the other. This creates the warm humid atmosphere that encourages the growth of discharge-forming organisms. So wear cotton pants and avoid wearing tights if you can.
- Don't use bubble baths and heavily perfumed bath oils, bath salts and soaps, all of which can irritate the fragile skin of the genital area and lower its resistance to organisms. So can the usual household disinfectants, and the sprays and aerosols which are suggested for these areas 'to keep you fresh'.
- Do use only the purest unscented soap to wash the genital area. The best thing to put in bath water is a handful of cooking salt.

- Do go and see a doctor if a discharge persists and ask him if your partner needs treatment too.

Lack of oestrogen at the time of the menopause can also cause dryness and cracking of the skin within the vagina. I described this in Chapter 6.

Vaginismus is a spasm of the muscles of the lower third of the vagina which is so powerful that it can prevent penetration. If penetration succeeds it may have had to be so forceful that it causes considerable pain. It is usually a problem that affects women in the earlier stages of their sex life and there can be greater or lesser degrees of spasm. Usually, of course, gentle and loving foreplay with a partner who is prepared to take things slowly can ease and eventually overcome the condition. Some women find that once penetration has occurred, even if it has been somewhat painful, they can relax and enjoy the later stages of love-making.

For some women, however, the muscle spasm is so complete and uncontrollable that full sexual activity is impossible and it is easy to see that the pain and fear caused by a man who does not understand why his partner appears to fear and reject him creates a vicious circle.

This condition will only crop up in middle age either if you have never had a physical relationship with a man before or if you have been through some experience that has made sex unpleasant or painful. In the first case, your normal bodily response, designed to protect you from penetration before your body is ready, is being triggered off unnecessarily. The second case is nearly always the result of physically and emotionally painful sexual intercourse, and sometimes of traumatic childbirth. Any of the conditions causing painful sexual intercourse, however, may make you back away and tighten up below, leading to secondary vaginismus.

The treatment for both types, which I shall describe later in this chapter, is similar and will depend upon discovering if there is any reason for the fear and anxiety that triggers off the spasm, eliminating the sources of pain, and teaching you how to relax the muscles of the lower end of the vagina.

Conditions affecting the internal sexual organs

Diseases of the sexual organs can affect all parts of the reproductive system, and cause, for example, fibroids in the uterus, cancer or infection of the cervix, or ovarian cysts and infections of the Fallopian tubes. They are likely to produce other symptoms that will be unpleasant enough for you to seek advice from your doctor, and sexual intercourse is probably only one instance in which you feel pain or discomfort. Rarely, it can be the first sign, and in this case you should be examined by your doctor. It is always better, though, to have regular check-ups, which will eliminate the chance of many of the problems becoming serious.

A prolapse caused by the slackness of the pelvic muscles after childbirth and the consequent sagging of the bladder and uterus into the vaginal space, or the bulging of the rectum or back passage into that same space, can sometimes cause discomfort during intercourse. As muscles become slack in the middle years anyway, you can see that a prolapse can become more troublesome as you get older and it may give rise to symptoms of back pain and a dragging sensation in the lower abdomen. Try the pelvic floor exercises on page 68, but if the condition is too pronounced to be improved this way, your doctor can insert a rubber or plastic ring or pessary into the top of the vaginal space; this is a simple process which, though slightly uncomfortable, requires no anaesthetic. If the condition is more serious, he may recommend an operation for tightening up the pelvic muscles.

Acute retroversion of the uterus   The uterus, or womb, is a fairly mobile organ within the abdominal cavity. Its usual position is tipped forward, but it can stand upright or tip backwards. When it tips backwards it is called a retroversion of the uterus. Out of about every ten women I see at clinic perhaps one will be found to have a retroversion. By her next visit her uterus will usually be tipped forward or upright. Retroversion is pretty frequent and usually causes no problems whatsoever. However, just occasionally the retroversion becomes acute and the uterus seems to get almost wedged backwards between the back passage and the back wall of the vagina and causes discomfort and dragging sensations very similar to those of a prolapse, with which this condition is often linked.

In the past three or four years I have seen about half a dozen women with retroversion of the uterus who also complained of considerable pain on deep thrusting by their partners during intercourse. No other cause was discovered for the pain and when the condition was treated (see below) they had no further trouble. With one exception, they were all women in their late thirties or forties.

I suspect that there are quite a few women who have temporary retroversion of the uterus who also experience occasional discomfort during intercourse, but who do not worry about it because it so seldom happens. Treatment is simple. During a vaginal examination the doctor can push the body of the uterus upwards and forwards. This will not always mean the uterus will stay there, but you will then be taught the knee-elbow exercise described on page 50, and encouraged to use it several times a day. You will also find the position of lying above your partner in intercourse more comfortable, partly because it helps to keep the uterus tipped forward and partly because it gives you greater control over the depth of your partner's thrusting movements. Just occasionally acute retroversion is associated with a degree of prolapse that makes surgery necessary, but this was not so in the women I have mentioned.

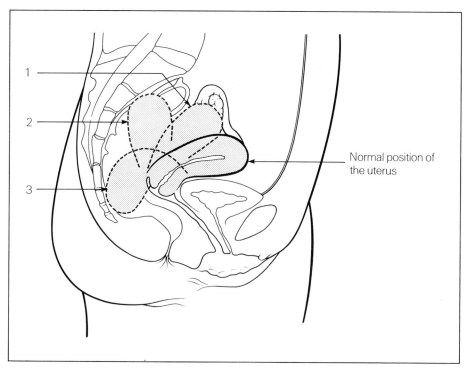

1

2

Normal position of
the uterus

3

Degrees of retroversion of the uterus.

Conditions that affect organs close to the genital area

Haemorrhoids (piles) and cystitis
These have been referred to already in Chapter 5; there are a number of good creams and suppositories your pharmacist could recommend. If the complaint is in any way severe, though, do consult your doctor.

What can be done about painful intercourse?
I will deal with the treatment for all the conditions that cause painful sexual intercourse together, since they are all so closely linked.

1. You should consult your family doctor or the doctor at a contraceptive clinic if intercourse becomes regularly painful, or even impossible.

2. You should try to identify for yourself, and then tell the doctor, exactly what happens during intercourse and when it becomes painful or impossible. Try to remember when you first noticed the problem and decide if it seems to be associated with any particular event: just

before a period, for example, or when you lie beneath rather than above your partner during sex, or when you are constipated.

3. You will be checked and treated for any of the physical conditions affecting the vagina, the sexual organs and other organs close to the genital area which I have already mentioned. This will undoubtedly involve an internal examination, which in the process will also reveal if there is evidence of vaginismus.

4. Once possible causes of pain and fear have been treated, treatment for vaginismus can begin. You will be helped to understand the causes for the pain that triggered off the spasm of vaginal muscles and to see that since these causes are now eliminated, this protective mechanism is no longer necessary. The following exercises – for use when being examined internally and at home – will help you to bring the tendency to spasm under control.
   - While you are encouraged to relax a further gentle examination will often show that a finger can be introduced into the vagina without undue discomfort.

You can help yourself to control vaginismus by slipping a finger into the vagina and relaxing and tightening the muscles which surround the lower third.

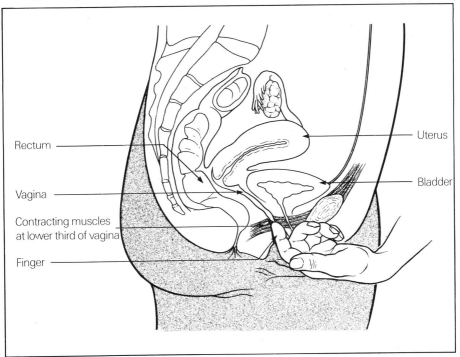

Rectum

Vagina

Contracting muscles
at lower third of vagina

Finger

Uterus

Bladder

- While the examiner's finger is in the vagina you will be encouraged to tighten up around it and to relax, and, if possible, to experience the trigger mechanism of vaginismus that sometimes occurs when sudden movements are made around the entrance to the vagina. You can then begin to identify the sudden spasm of the muscles, which you can be taught to get under control.
- You will then be encouraged to practise examining yourself with one or more fingers suitably lubricated, moving your finger around so that you can feel the muscles slacken off around the finger. You are instructed to tighten and relax the muscles of the lower third of the vagina until you feel this effect on your finger, and gradually to get this loosening and tightening to happen under your control.
- The use of so-called dilators can be useful. Dilators are short, smooth, rounded lengths of metal or plastic ranging in diameter from small finger size to a size larger than the diameter of any penis. I don't like the name, for it implies stretching and what I want you to achieve is relaxation. Stretching implies that the mouth of the vagina is too tight because it is made that way or has become so physically; relaxing implies that the opening up of the vaginal entrance is perfectly possible if you exercise conscious control of your muscles. Insertion of a dilator, in this case, is not forcing something open, but simply measuring the degree of muscle relaxation you can achieve. Think of the muscles around your mouth. If you purse them up tightly and try and force your finger through it is quite painful. If you relax them there is plenty of room!

5. Most cases of vaginismus do not have severe underlying emotional causes and are not difficult to treat, once the physical conditions causing the pain are cleared up. There are situations, of course, where pain, anxiety and shutting yourself up against sex are the result of situations that have affected you emotionally and these can have an effect on the way you react physically. They may be caused by circumstances not connected with your partner, a bereavement, for example, or a painful previous sexual encounter, or they may be due to other difficulties within your relationship. These may have to be dealt with in several counselling sessions, possibly with a marriage counsellor, before you will be ready even to contemplate the physical vaginal exercises described above. It is foolish to attempt them until you are happy enough with your relationship with your partner to want to do so. Then he will supply the final part of the treatment.

6. Gentle introduction of the penis into the vagina is this final stage. It cannot be rushed and the important thing for your partner to understand is that it must be under your control, certainly at first. Full penetration can be achieved only as you feel confident about it.

Failure of orgasm

Failure of orgasm is different from lack of interest – which I shall cover in the next section. You may be interested in sex, want it, be happy with foreplay, have no fear of penetration, enjoy being touched and yet be unable to have an orgasm. Orgasm is something you may never have experienced, or only occasionally and with difficulty. Some women are quite content with this situation and for many people this seems to be a quite usual variation in sexual response. However, this may well be something that develops in middle age and can cause a feeling of loss or of fading femininity.

How orgasm is achieved

The spark that sets off orgasm in the woman is situated in the clitoris, the small firm nodule that lies at the top and front of the cleft formed by the fleshy lips that enclose the genital area. This is the trigger mechanism for orgasm, and it can be stimulated either directly by the fingers, or by the movements of intercourse, or by pulling on the muscles of the hood that surrounds it, which is achieved by the entrance and thrusting of the penis in the vagina. Orgasm itself can be located simply in and directly around the clitoris itself or can involve spasmodic contractions of all the muscles in and around the vagina, and even jerking movements throughout the whole of the lower abdomen, thighs and back. It is all a question of degree, and not only do individual women differ from each other, but also at different times they may experience different degrees of orgasm. It is important to say that there doesn't seem to be a set way or frequency of orgasm. If what you have suits you, that's fine!

How to overcome the problem with manual stimulation

There is, however, one aspect about which I find there is often considerable ignorance here that does need explaining. The manipulation of the hood of the clitoris by vaginal penetration is not an efficient way of stimulating the clitoris. Often the movements both couples make during love-making are not efficient stimulators either. Some women find that different positions in intercourse, such as the position of the woman on top, cause more stimulation, but others don't seem to find any really satisfactory position to obtain this stimulation.

If you add to this that many people are brought up to feel that they shouldn't touch themselves in the genital area, or be touched by their partner, then obviously the clitoris may never get the stimulation it needs. Moreover, many people I have spoken to feel that it shouldn't be necessary to use the hands to obtain this stimulation – that the man should be able to satisfy his partner without manual help. If you could only be encouraged to masturbate while making love you would discover you could reach orgasm fairly easily, and you could also do so if your partner stimulated you.

It is easy to see that here you both need to be helped. You will need to:

1. Accept that it is fairly common for sexual movements, even penetration, not to stimulate the clitoris.
2. Try other positions to see if they will help.
3. Come to terms with genital touching, either by yourself or your partner.
4. Learn how to stimulate the clitoris manually during intercourse to help achieve orgasm.

Sometimes in middle age, change in your shape or size or difficulty in getting into certain positions may prevent stimulation of the clitoris where previously it was easily achieved. Sometimes, for example, slackness of the vaginal muscles may cause this loss. You can be reassured that this is not uncommon, so try to explore other methods, including manual stimulation. At first you may be reluctant to change to manual methods which you have not used before, even to masturbation on your own. The point is, that once you have achieved an orgasm, by whatever methods, you will realize that there is nothing faulty with your physical response, only that it needs a different method of stimulation from before. This is very similar to the need of some men for increased stimulation as they get older to achieve a satisfactory erection.

What if manual stimulation doesn't work?
Sometimes you will find that even manual stimulation will not produce an orgasm. Here you will have to find out what is the inhibiting or 'turn-off' factor. As I explained in Chapter 2, it may be due to learned attitudes, or holding back, or other reasons. A vibrator can be useful here. This is a small electrical device that emits a rapid throb, the frequency of which can be altered, and which can be applied either to the clitoris or to the inside of the vagina. The stimulation this provides can often get through the inhibiting barrier and cause an orgasm. Once you have achieved this and found orgasm to be possible, you can continue with efforts to reach one again, with or without the vibrator. It can be used by you on your own or during intercourse. You will need to work together patiently to help each other. Don't be put off: success sometimes takes several weeks or months, and there may be setbacks on the way.

General lack of interest in sex

Some women never seem to have been able to respond sexually in any way. They do not enjoy physical contact, nor do they respond to efforts to arouse them; they do not lubricate nor do they feel any response to touching the genital area or to penetration; they do not have an orgasm.

This absolute inability to respond sexually is usually discovered when a woman first starts a relationship with a man, and it can, of course, cause a great deal of difficulty in that relationship. It is unlikely that this primary type of lack of interest – primary because it has its sources far back in a woman's life – will be something that will present itself in the middle years. You will either have sought help already or worked out with your partner ways in which you will both be happy about sex.

When all interest fades
A second type of lack of interest in sex occurs in a woman who has been able to respond with at least some excitement to sex, but gradually, or occasionally quite suddenly, is unable to do so at any level. There are many variations on this theme, but to a greater or lesser extent women who suffer in this way find that all their sexual responses are diminished or fade away altogether. Sometimes sex becomes not merely uninteresting or non-arousing, but positively objectionable. They may reach the stage where they find that even the touch of their partner's hand provokes a feeling of repugnance and withdrawal.

In the same way that 'impotence' is a word hurled at men as an insult, so is 'frigidity' at women. Now some women with this overall disinterest in or revulsion against sex are cold, but the distressing part for many is that they are in other ways warm and loving towards their partners and are as upset as their partners about their inability to respond. Because of this, many of them carry a great burden of guilt.

When it happens in the middle years
Unfortunately, the lack of interest in sex often surfaces during the middle years because of other pressures (see Chapter 4). Often when children finally leave home and the couple have more time to themselves, the woman, and perhaps the man too, begins to realize that though he may still enjoy intercourse she is developing a total lack of interest and response.

Many of you may have experienced short periods when you don't really feel like sex, but this may develop into something much more permanent. It can upset you a lot and often cause distress and even anger in your partner, who may feel you are simply not interested in him. No matter how hard you try, there isn't the faintest spark there.

Can lack of interest be treated?
Treatment of this condition often takes some time, for the woman concerned has to be helped to understand how it arose; then to work with her partner so that both can see what each has contributed to the situation and to explore how they can change, and finally to put the changes into effect.

Both partners do need to seek help to understand and remodel their sex lives together.

The case of Mary, a woman of fifty-four, is typical of the secondary type of lack of interest in sex. When I saw her she said, 'Quite frankly, I wouldn't mind if we never had sex again, but it's so unfair on my husband. We are the greatest of friends and we enjoy doing things together and he still wants me, but I find the whole process boring. I used to pretend that I enjoyed it – but I'm getting so that I actually dislike intercourse. It doesn't do anything for me. The awful thing is that when my husband goes off on business trips, I actually give a sigh of relief and enjoy being in bed on my own. It sounds awful, doesn't it? He has realized for some time that I'm – well not exactly enthusiastic, and I don't want to hurt him.'

She went on to tell me of her anxieties. Was it her age? Did women fade out, so to speak, sooner than men? Ought she to continue to pretend she enjoyed sex? Was there anything abnormal about her? Ought she to grin and bear it for her husband's sake? and so on.

Whatever had been the underlying cause of her loss of response, it was now overlaid with all sorts of other feelings of anxiety and guilt. 'I would quite understand if he found himself a younger and more exciting woman', was her final remark.

Mary's husband, Derek, was fifty-six. They had a grown-up family who had now left home. She said she was completely uninterested in sex and had a great many anxieties about the situation, not the least being that she was afraid that her husband might turn to another woman. Mary and I started to work together and this is what we discovered.

She had been brought up by loving but strict parents. She had one older brother and no sisters and she had grown up feeling that men were the important people and that women were there to support and cherish them. This was the pattern in her parents' harmonious marriage. Her mother was a perfect housewife, and though Mary remembered her father as affectionate and generous, he was very much master in his own house. She saw her childhood as being calm and happy, and though both parents were now dead, she remembered them with love and deep respect. She still maintained a friendly relationship with her brother and his family. If she had the least criticism of her mother it was that she never discussed anything sexual openly. This is not to say that she didn't make sure that Mary knew the facts of life – but even when Mary tried to open things up between them just before she got married, her mother's reply was to smile and say, 'I'm sure Derek and you will find out things together. That's a husband's privilege, and I'm sure you will be able to please him.'

Mary was deeply in love with Derek, who had a successful career in banking. He fitted in well with her family. She had herself been trained in domestic science and catering and before her marriage had worked at a small restaurant run by two of her friends. She gave this up when she got married, though very occasionally she went back to give her friends a hand when they were busy with some special function. It also emerged, under questioning, that Mary was a fine needlewoman and embroideress, but she didn't consider this as anything to be particularly proud of. She kept saying that she wasn't brainy.

At first, though intercourse was slightly painful – 'I was very tight down below' – she enjoyed love-making. Derek was passionate and kind and she found his closeness very exciting. She said, however, that often she did not have an orgasm. In fact, she said, she didn't really know what to expect and didn't really miss it. It was not that Derek rushed her, in fact foreplay was the most pleasant part for her, though he never touched her genitals much, and had never stimulated her clitoris manually. 'I think he knew I was a bit embarrassed if he did.' It was then that she began to pretend. They never spoke during intercourse, but she realized that sometimes when he had penetrated, he seemed to be holding back and waiting for her, 'So I used to indicate that I was ready when I really wasn't. I felt I oughtn't to stop his continued pleasure – and it was so obvious that he enjoyed it.' Sometimes she was left feeling tense and frustrated, but mostly she accepted the situation.

Mary's three children were born at fairly close intervals, but the last birth was rather rapid and she had a nasty tear which left her sore and uncomfortable below. Derek was very understanding and intercourse was not resumed for some time, and then less frequently. As this coincided with bringing up three lively children and increasing business responsibilities for Derek, they both took it as natural. However, from this time onwards Mary hardly ever achieved an orgasm, and then only after prolonged stimulation. Still she said nothing to Derek.

The years bringing up the family were happy ones. The house was always full of youngsters, they both enjoyed entertaining and Mary was a tower of strength on local committees, besides finding time to fill the house with her lovely embroidered cushions and chair seats. They were often tired and love-making when it occurred was brief and less and less exciting for Mary.

It was just after her elder daughter's wedding when Mary was forty-eight, that she had a bad dose of flu followed by painful cystitis (see page 56) which seemed to drag on. After that she found herself very unwilling to have intercourse at all. She forced herself for Derek's sake – 'and I hope he didn't realize that I didn't really want it.'

Since then, things had gone from bad to worse for her. She seemed to have a lot of headaches through the menopause and a feeling of abdominal fullness which again made sex uncomfortable. She had been for examination and a cervical smear, but nothing abnormal was found.

At last Derek had openly asked her why she no longer enjoyed love-making. She had really prevaricated, talked about the change and cystitis and tiredness and had felt very guilty about spoiling his pleasure. She assured him of her love and he seemed to understand but said, 'I still want you so badly, it seems funny that you no longer need me.' She knew then that all the pretending in the past was working against her. 'How could I tell him that I hadn't enjoyed it for a long time?'

Mary's story shows very clearly the sort of elements that combine to develop loss of feeling in later life. Her upbringing which, though it may have been loving and caring, was strict, that is it set high standards, and suggested that men were important and women there to serve them. It was also implied that sex was something you didn't discuss and that the man set the tone and the woman strove to please. Her opinion of herself was that she wasn't clever and she didn't really value even the things she was good at. She saw herself very much as the junior partner in the marriage: her role was to safeguard her husband's well-being and happiness.

The person she married was very similar to her father, whom she loved and respected, and within his understanding he loved and cherished her – but wasn't all that sensitive to her feelings. Her view of sex was that it was important for her husband, and that is was in his interest and therefore better to pretend than to admit that she didn't enjoy it. Consequently, her sexual needs were neither discussed nor considered important.

Her involvement with her family, friends and outside interests took up enough of her energy to compensate at first for diminishing sexual enjoyment, but gradually the situation became worse. An illness which created discomfort around the genital area made sexual activity not merely non-arousing, but actually painful and the menopause and its side-effects reinforced her distaste for sexual contact.

Good sex was not something that Mary felt she could demand, or expect, or even need. She took no responsibility for herself as a sexual being except as a necessary part of her husband's enjoyment. Guilt was a strong element in her reactions. 'You must think me awful – I feel that I'm not really a good wife.' Over-compensation made her try so hard to respond, to conceal her lack of enjoyment, to make sure her husband's pleasure wasn't diminished, that things went from bad to worse because of the anxiety and stress she felt. Hidden anger was very hard to elicit. In the end when she began to accept that she had really been a very good wife, she was able to say that she had been hurt when she found that her husband hadn't even realized that she hadn't enjoyed sex for some time.

What can be done to help this lack of feeling?
Mary and I talked a lot together and I saw her several times before we asked her husband to join us. I have quoted Mary's case at length because there is much in it that will be of value to many people.

Seek help   She asked for help. This is a tremendous step to take and can be very frightening. You aren't sure how the person you talk to will respond, you feel embarrassed, you feel stupid and inadequate, and you probably feel that this has never happened to anyone else or at any rate not in such an acute form.

Acknowledge your own value, especially sexually   Mary began to see how she had been 'set up' by her upbringing and the attitudes instilled into her to behave in this way. During counselling she was encouraged to acknowledge that she had a value too, that she had her own skills and had made her own special contributions which had benefited the marriage and the family. She began to accept that she had her own needs and feelings in the sexual field which were as important as her husband's and which in the long run would make love-making better for both of them. She was helped to take a more confident attitude to her own sexuality. When her husband, Derek, came to join us, we looked at several areas:

Start to communicate with each other   Communication between Mary and Derek had not been good and there had been many of those small wordless signs between them that had been missed: her apparent tiredness, her lack of demand, and so on. Derek began to understand why she had 'deceived' him, and to see that, however mistakenly, she meant it for the best; and then he realized that he had to take some responsibility for his lack of sensitivity. This led in turn to his feeling guilty.

Don't blame each other   With help, they began to see that putting blame on each other or themselves was not really constructive, but accepting the obligation to change and thinking what they could do about it was.

Take positive steps about changing patterns of sex   Having dealt with these preliminary problems, we then began to work together to see what could be done to alter the situation. They became more honest with each other and were able to say what in love-making they wanted or liked and what they didn't. They both understood that things would have to change and that the changes might require effort on both sides. Mary knew that Derek still wanted sex fairly frequently, so she decided that she had to take some initiatives if Derek was to know that she was prepared to accept his need.

You, as the woman, must accept responsibility   So, we agreed that for the moment Mary would be in control. I suggested that temporarily they should agree not to go to full intercourse, so that they would never feel pressurized. They agreed – but Mary said, 'It's really up to me, isn't it?' Derek laughed and said, 'Yes, your turn now, – I think I shall enjoy that!'
This stage took several weeks. Mary found it very difficult to take the lead and in turn became angry when Derek didn't respond to faint signals, such as suggesting that they went to bed early, and panic-stricken when he responded 'like a takeover bid'. By degrees she began to enjoy the gentle cuddling sessions. Derek sometimes got quite angry, 'She isn't really trying.' 'How long is all this nonsense going on?' But everyone kept trying.
Mary gradually became more confident – even confident enough to say,

'Sorry, not tonight, I really am tired.'

In fact the 'cure' came quite suddenly after a celebration – one of their birthdays, I think. They had been out for a quiet meal together, driven home not too late, and had both suddenly been overwhelmed with a desire for each other. There was no mistaking the signals on either side and, in fact, though Derek paused a moment to ask if Mary was 'ready', there was never any doubt that both were now eager and excited.

They came in smiling and Mary was almost blushing as they told me.

Don't worry about occasional setbacks I had to warn them not to be put off if they had setbacks, but they had learnt to accept what each felt able to give at any one time and not to see a gentle 'no more' or 'not tonight' as a rebuff. In fact, what they found was that they did enjoy the preliminary stages far more than they had done previously. They also enjoyed talking to each other and telling each other when some aspect of caressing was particularly pleasant. They no longer felt that no sex means no loving and again discovered and treasured some of the other ways that each tried to care for the other.

Each sexual problem has its own special solution

Not all situations end quite as quickly or as simply as this. Sometimes the difficulties that have divided a couple have bitten so deep that one may find it hard to trust or to accept the other, but if each is prepared to see what he or she has contributed to the problem and to try to readjust to suit the other, people can be helped to work through such difficulties.

Perhaps the description of this case and the way Mary and Derek were able to work with me to sort things out will encourage you to seek help from a trained sexual counsellor if you have seemingly insoluble sexual problems. There may not be a simple magic cure, but if you can both come with a willingness to try and work through difficulties, a counsellor can help you to uncover the reasons why you developed the problem in the first place and advise you how to tackle it – opening the way for you to enjoy sex together more, and to deepen and enhance your total relationship.

9 CONTRACEPTION: CHANGING NEEDS IN THE MIDDLE YEARS

Changing methods

Some women complete their families before they are thirty; others prefer to continue with their careers, or to save for a house and furniture, and postpone starting their family until their early thirties; but most women in the Western world do not want babies after their early forties. They may still have ten to twelve years before the menopause and though their fertility decreases during this time, there is still a strong possibility of pregnancy occurring if sexual intercourse takes place with no contraceptive control.

There are, of course, some women who from personal choice or religious reasons are content to have babies for as long and as often as it is possible. If this is what you feel, this chapter is not written for you. If both husband and wife are happy with this situation, then, of course, there is no problem.

For every one of you who feels this way, however, there are many in the middle years who become really anxious at the thought of an unwanted pregnancy and the problem is made greater by the fact that certainly by the time you are forty some forms of contraceptives are not suitable for you and you may have to consider other methods. This is still a comparatively new phenomenon, which arises from the fact that women are now coming to their middle years who have never used any other method of contraception than the Pill, or oral contraceptive. For many of you this has been a simple and trouble-free method and you have not had to bother with any other devices that require more than just the act of swallowing. Up to now you have had almost complete security for very little trouble; you have been able to plan and space your family according to your wishes, your health and your financial situation, and you may view a change of method with anxiety and distaste.

If you are still on even the mini-pill (see page 105) at the time of the menopause, you will have to stop using it to make sure when the menopause is complete, and during this hiatus you will probably be advised to use other methods until you are sure that all risk of pregnancy is over.

Whose responsibility?

While the decision to plan a family may be taken by both partners, the actual responsibility for carrying it through is frequently taken by the woman. Her partner, up until middle age, may seldom, if ever, have had to bother about doing anything himself. Many men are quite content to leave contraceptive planning to their wives, especially if they feel that they are attending either their family doctor or a clinic who will keep an expert eye on their wife's suitability for, and health on, the Pill.

The male options
Many men, too, with increasing pressure from work, finance and a growing young family, won't want any more children, but because up to now the responsibility for contraception has seldom been theirs, they may not quite understand the problem. They may not appreciate that after so long a change in method is necessary. They may feel that the chances of having a child are really much lower than they are supposed to be and not take at all kindly to having to use a sheath (condom) or to having a vasectomy (male sterilization). Often the change of method is seen as still being the woman's responsibility and sometimes sexual difficulties such as not reaching an orgasm and reluctance for sex can be directly related to a woman's increasing anxiety about pregnancy and her anger that she is again left, metaphorically, and actually, to 'carry the baby'.

Of course, there are many men who are interested and who are prepared to take a full share of responsibility for contraception, but my experience, after more than twenty-five years in family-planning clinics is that they are not in the majority. Much of this attitude is not malicious, but is due to a lack of knowledge about the risks and the methods, so I shall now consider the various possibilities with their pros and cons.

Examining the possibilities
The suitability of any one method of contraception depends not only on personal choice, but also on your physical make-up and your previous medical history. Since individual responses vary so greatly, the only sensible thing to do is to go and discuss all the possibilities fully with either your family doctor or your neighbourhood clinic. Preferably both you and your partner should go and discuss the situation together so that you can both share in the decision about methods.

Commonly used methods that are unreliable

Abstinence (the rhythm method or 'safe period')
Total abstinence is, of course, the method which is entirely reliable if you

want to avoid pregnancy – but hardly likely to commend itself to most of you. However, many people cut down on the frequency of intercourse and many more use the so-called 'safe period'. At best this method ought to be called the 'only-slightly-safer period'. It depends on the fact that for many women the shedding of the egg from the ovary occurs roughly midway in their regular menstrual cycle, and that if this time is avoided with an overlap of two to three days on each side, there will be no egg available to be fertilized, and so no pregnancy.

What it involves It is true that with very regular periods and a series of recorded morning temperatures you can identify the most likely time of ovulation for yourself and can then make the necessary calculations to identify the time when sex is to be avoided. This method can be explained to you in detail at your contraceptive clinic. It is particularly unsatisfactory for the woman who is approaching the menopause, since her periods may become so irregular that it is difficult to be exact about the critical time.

It also takes no account of so-called 'sporadic' ovulation; this is when the ovaries can produce an extra egg during a single menstrual cycle outside the normal time. It seems that this can sometimes be triggered by the act of intercourse. This accounts for pregnancies which have occurred – and I have knowledge of several – where the only act of intercourse that could have produced a pregnancy was either immediately after or before the period.

It is therefore not a method I would recommend, especially during the middle years.

Withdrawal, or coitus interruptus

Withdrawal involves the man removing his penis from the vagina before he ejaculates. This is a notoriously unreliable method as even the smallest drop of seminal fluid may contain a great number of sperms. Surprisingly, though, it is still widely practised. There is another fairly obvious disadvantage to this method which is that often one or other partner is not fully satisfied – the woman in particular may not have reached orgasm. Since your responses get slower the older you get, you may both find it more difficult to enjoy your sex life to the full using this method.

I have mentioned both these methods not because I consider either of them to be appropriate means of birth control, but because they are still used by so many and because, as people get older, both methods actually become less reliable and less pleasurable.

There are a considerable number of far more reliable contraceptive methods that will enable you not only to feel secure that you will not have an unwanted pregnancy, but will also allow you to enjoy sexual intercourse to the full. They each have their advantages and disadvantages related to the middle years.

Recommended methods for women

The Pill, or oral contraceptive

The Pill depends on its effect on hormones which prevent the ovary from producing eggs. Introduced about twenty years ago, it is now by far the most popular method of contraception used by women, although it is used less by women in middle age than in the younger age group (see below). It is about 99 per cent effective as a contraceptive. This simple method, which involves taking a pill once a day, either for twenty-one days with a subsequent gap of seven days before starting the next twenty-one-day cycle, or regularly every day, has revolutionized birth control. You may start the cycle on the first or the fifth day of your period, depending on what is recommended for you.

Constant research over the past twenty years or so has produced a wide variety of compounds that have combined an ever-greater reliability of contraception with an ever-increasing safety factor and a lessening of side-effects. However, there are dangers and there are side-effects and these will vary from woman to woman.

Possible side-effects I do not want to go into extensive details of all these. They will be discussed with you by the doctor concerned wherever the oral contraceptive is not available without a prescription.

The danger most closely related to the middle years is thrombosis. To have a thrombosis means to have a blood clot that settles in a blood vessel in the body. It can be quite mild, like a clot in the vein of a leg, or it can be severe, like a clot in the heart – a coronary thrombosis. The chance of your being injured in a car accident is very much higher than the chance of having a severe thrombosis while on the Pill, but thromboses can be fatal, and even a minor one should be taken as a warning if you are on the Pill.

Anyone can have a thrombosis of course, not just those on the oral contraceptive. Certain factors will increase their likelihood though. These are:

1. Increase in age.
2. Too great an increase in weight.
3. Too great an increase in blood pressure.
4. Smoking, especially cigarettes.
5. Pregnancy.
6. The Pill.

You can see that as you reach the middle years the first three are likely to go up slightly – and the combination of any or all of them with smoking, plus being on the oral contraceptive, can add to the risks. No one wants to add an extra factor if it can be avoided and this is why most people are taken off the Pill by the age of forty, and sometimes considerably earlier if they are subject to any of the factors I have listed.

Of the other side-effects of the Pill, one or two are of special importance in the middle years. One is that it may, in a few cases, cause loss of desire and a general disinterest in sex. Occasionally it can also worsen depression and increase the number of headaches.

Cutting the risks   There are now varieties of Pill that carry less risk. Most pills consist of two hormones, oestrogen and progesterone, of which oestrogen is the more likely to cause thrombosis. Already the oestrogen content has been lowered in nearly every type without loss of contraceptive effectiveness. Now there are progesterone-only pills, known as the 'mini-pill' which have eliminated the more harmful oestrogen while being only 1-2 per cent less effective as contraceptives.

Unfortunately recent research has shown that a small amount of progesterone can be converted into oestrogen in the body.

I cannot emphasize too strongly that the risks are still very slight and that they have to be balanced anyway with risks that can occur in pregnancies for the over-forties. Anyone prescribing the Pill has therefore to take a great many considerations into account.

Other problems   This easy method of contraception has caused difficulties for some people. Before the Pill, restricting the frequency of intercourse was one way of lessening the risk of pregnancy, and often, especially for people in middle age who were tired or under stress, it provided a natural reason for stopping love-making before penetration and ejaculation occurred. The Pill now makes women and consequently men available all the time, and this can cause considerable pressure if one partner would prefer not to have intercourse as frequently but finds it difficult to say no.

Taking the Pill is so easy that it has often made other methods of contraception seem distasteful and not as reliable, and when a woman has to change methods in middle age for health reasons, it can cause a degree of tension over sex.

So to sum up, there are several points to remember if you are on the Pill:

1. You should have regular check-ups, including having your weight and blood pressure and your general health assessed.

2. If your check-ups show a progressive increase in weight and blood pressure, and you also smoke, these are indications to stop taking the Pill.

3. There are occasional side-effects which can affect sex in the middle years.

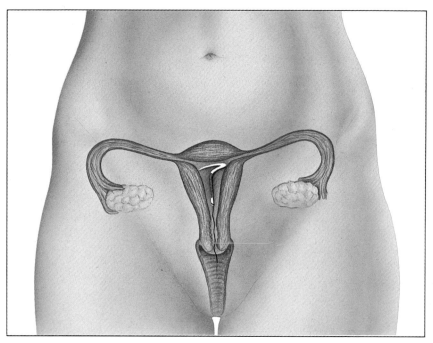

The Copper-7 variety of the intra-uterine device in expanded position within the cavi
of the uterus, showing the 'check-strings'.

The cap in position in the vagina, showing how it covers the neck of the uterus.

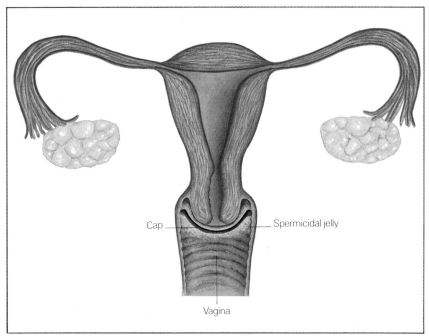

4. If the above risks do not apply to you, you should be able to take the Pill until you are thirty-five. Many women can take it until they're forty, but only under careful supervision.

5. When you are over forty, the progesterone-only pill is a possible alternative. It has one or two disadvantages, however:
   - It has to be taken every day at the same time of day, with no break, to be effective.
   - Sometimes your period loss on this type of pill can be heavy, lengthy and irregular.
   - Some progesterone can be converted into oestrogen in the body.
   - On all oral contraceptives, including this one, the only sure test of whether the menopause is complete is to come off the Pill and see. Obviously, if normal periods return the menopause is not complete and risk of pregnancy is still present, though reduced.
   - It is not as reliable a contraceptive as the combined Pill – though it is probably as effective, or more so, than any other method.

What about the 'morning-after' pill? It has recently been found that when intercourse takes place without the use of contraceptives, and very high doses of the combined contraceptive pill are taken within seventy-two hours of the event, contraception may be prevented. Even so, this method has certain strong disadvantages attached to it.

1. At present two pills must be taken as soon as possible after intercourse and another two twelve hours later, all within seventy-two hours of intercourse.
2. It may cause intense nausea.
3. It is not totally effective and we do not know yet what this high dose of hormones might do to the foetus.
4. High doses of oestrogen increase the risk of thrombosis.

Research is still being carried out on the effect of this method, so it is too early to recommend it with total confidence.

The intra-uterine device (IUD)
This is often called 'the coil' but an IUD can also be a shield or a T-shaped device. Basically it is a shaped piece of plastic or metal which is introduced into the uterus. Insertion is a quick and simple procedure which must be performed only by your doctor or at a contraceptive clinic and which requires no anaesthetic. It prevents the embedding of the fertilized egg in the wall of the uterus so that pregnancy does not develop. In my experience, about 12 per cent of all women using contraception have the IUD.

This is a method which is more suitable for women who have had babies. The different types have been developed throughout the world. Your doctor will choose which she feels would be the most effective for you. IUDs are nearly always inserted during a period. Two fine strands of plastic attached to the device hang down outside the mouth of the cervix.

Pros and cons Its advantage is that it is a once-for-all procedure which if successful remains in position for several years and prevents pregnancies. Its position can be checked fairly easily by feeling the 'strings' below the cervix. In any event, you should have a check-up about once in two years in case the IUD needs changing for any reason.

It has, however, certain disadvantages. Some people cannot retain the device and it is simply rejected, whatever kind is used. For some women it can cause rather heavy and sometimes painful periods and occasionally dragging back pain. It isn't quite as reliable a contraceptive as the Pill – around 95 per cent effective, in fact. If your periods are heavy and irregular anyway and if, perhaps with some increase in weight, or slackness of the muscles, back ache is already a problem – all possible in middle age – the IUD may not be the right choice for you.

The cap, or diaphragm

It is my experience as a doctor and counsellor that the cap can be a very useful contraceptive method for the middle aged. Intelligently used according to the rules I shall list, it will have none of the side-effects of the other methods and has a high reliability rate – close to that of the mini-pill and the IUD. The cap or diaphragm is exactly what it says it is, a thin cap of rubber mounted on a circular rubber-coated spring which can be introduced into the vagina to cover the neck of the womb or cervix. There are one or two other varieties, but this is the most usual one. Sensibly used, the success rate of the cap is about 96 per cent.

You insert it yourself before intercourse, making sure that it covers the neck of the womb, and remove it not less than six hours after intercourse.

The points for It acts with the help of a sperm-killing cream by covering the entrance to the uterus and preventing sperms reaching the eggs. It has one very strong advantage over other methods for women, especially in middle age, in that it doesn't affect the body in any other way than by being a mechanical barrier to sperm. It doesn't interfere with hormones; it doesn't affect periods; and, provided it is correctly sized and fitted, it cannot be felt by either partner during intercourse. You can see that while the Pill may cause problems of various sorts when you are over forty and the IUD may upset periods which may already be irregular and heavy with the approaching menopause, the cap has none of these disadvantages.

The points against It has, however, had rather bad publicity – the so-called cap failures. I prefer to call them human failures, for just as the Pill has to be taken regularly with regular check-ups, so the successful use of the cap involves keeping certain rules. They are fairly simple:

1. The cap must fit the individual and fitting must be done profession-ally, since there are many different sizes of cap and the right one for you can only be judged by a vaginal examination.
2. Regular check-ups – say, once every six months – are essential to make sure that the cap is still the right size and in good condition.
3. The cap must be inserted correctly so that it covers the cervix, and the user must learn to recognize the feel of the end of the cervix behind the rubber of the cap.
4. The cap must be used with spermicidal cream. Full instructions are given with the cap. Some people like to use a spermicidal pessary as well, especially if the cap has been in position some time before intercourse.
5. It must remain in position a minimum of six hours after intercourse, preferably a bit longer. If intercourse takes place again before the six hours are up, it is sensible to insert an extra spermicidal pessary and another six hours must elapse before the cap is removed.

One of the apparent drawbacks of going on to the cap after having been on the Pill is that it seems more complicated. You have to learn to introduce it yourself; and it seems messy, and perhaps more premeditated than the Pill. It really is worth consulting someone who will teach you how to use the cap, rather than trying to teach yourself from the instructions that come with it. If your family doctor does not provide this service, family planning or contraceptive clinics do. You will feel much more relaxed about using a cap if you have been shown how to and had your efforts checked. Remember, it can be a very successful contraceptive if you are not careless about it. Have it checked regularly: the size of your vagina does change, rubber does deteriorate in time, spermicidal cream is essential and takes time to be effective; but if you take account of these things you can look for success.

Make a habit of it   One other point is worth mentioning. If you wait until just before sexual intercourse, until you actually know it is going to happen, before you put your cap in – 'hold everything, dear, while I go and get the cap' – it can be a real passion-killer for you and your partner! This is especially true if either of you is a bit tired or finding it an effort to respond to love-making. That is often when the slip-ups occur – 'I just can't be bothered . . .'

The effective way to use the cap is to insert it every day regularly at some point when you have enough time to do it without hurrying. It should be like brushing your teeth or combing your hair – both of which I'm sure you do at some time before you go to bed. Then you can go through all the stages steadily as a routine that is not linked to whether or not you have intercourse that night.

Sterilization

Sterilization is another method of ensuring that conception cannot take place. This is done in women by tying off the Fallopian tubes on both sides of the uterus and so closing the passage through which the egg reaches the uterus. The eggs which are still released at ovulation simply fall into the body cavity and are absorbed, with no ill-effects at all, by the body tissues. Without being a major operation, and though new methods are constantly being perfected, it will mean that you have to have an operation under anaesthetic.

Some women find the finality of sterilization emotionally more than they can take. It is certainly something you and your partner have to be very sure about before you undertake it. Very few women I see – only two or three a year – go in for sterilization.

Abortion

I cannot end the list of female methods of contraception without mentioning abortion, now used by a rapidly growing number of women. As a method, it is at least a confession of failure of other methods and at best a safety net to deal with that failure. Technically, it is now a remarkably safe procedure with few complications on the physical side.

Emotionally, however, there is a different story. Of course, for many people it provides an escape from an unwanted pregnancy, which they clutch at thankfully. In my experience, however, it often leaves a scar of regret and guilt that can be all the more difficult to deal with, because it seems irrational and is therefore often suppressed. It can spill over into a disenchantment with sex and is often secretly blamed on the other partner. Either wife or husband may have privately longed for another child, however impractical this may have been, financially or in relation to the rest of the family. Preventing conception is one thing: actually disposing of a pregnancy is another.

I would not dissuade a couple who had decided abortion was the only way out, but I would ask them to think deeply about it, without rushing into panic decisions. I would ask them to be honest with each other and to come to terms with any feelings of guilt and blame that might remain, even if the decision to go ahead seemed in the end to be sensible and necessary. They may have to recognize that these feelings and others of anxiety about preventing a recurrence of this situation may spill over into their sex life.

Methods for men

Apart from withdrawal, which I have already discussed on page 101, there are only two methods in which the contraceptive responsibility lies with the man, the sheath and vasectomy.

The sheath (condom)

This is the commonest recommended method after the Pill. There are a great variety of sheaths, thin or thinner, differently tipped, lubricated or not. Some are actually prepared with a spermicidal lubricating film already on them. Those without have low contraceptive reliability unless they are used with spermicidal pessaries or cream inserted into the woman's vagina; then the success rate is about 91 per cent. The sheath acts as a barrier. In the same way that a cap prevents sperms entering the neck of the womb, so a sheath, by covering the penis, traps the sperms and prevents them getting into the vagina.

Some disadvantages A sheath is placed on the erect penis, so that the process of love-making has to be broken into at some stage. Because of this, and because the sheath also has to be removed at some time, there are two danger points, before and after, when sperms may enter the vagina; spermicidal cream or pessaries are needed as a second line of defence.

In the middle years this interruption of your love-making may create certain difficulties. If you find erection difficult to maintain for long, or if indeed it is occasionally difficult to achieve an erection at all, having to stop and put on a sheath can add to your problems. Similarly, if your partner finds it takes time to become aroused, the break may cause her to lose the urge. Anxiety about becoming pregnant may also make her unhappy about the sheath. Occasionally too, conditions of dryness or soreness in the vagina may be worsened by the added friction of a sheath.

Some men find that sheaths diminish sensation during intercourse and this may be especially noticeable for the older man who responds more slowly and requires greater stimulation. And some men find ready-lubricated sheaths messy and unpleasant to put on. There are many types, however, and with improved materials some are now 'gossamer' thin. It is worth trying different ones to discover which suits you best.

Vasectomy

Vasectomy is a quick and simple operation, performed under local anaesthetic, in which the tubes that bring the sperm from the testicles to the penis are cut and separated. Unlike sterilization in the woman, the abdominal cavity is not entered, which makes it a less severe procedure.

Technically and physically it has few disadvantages. The seminal vesicles, which produce the milky fluid that surrounds the sperms before the vasectomy, are well above the cut in the tubes and so continue to produce a fluid, now without sperm, which passes into the penis and is used in ejaculation. The act of sex is in no way interfered with though the fluid no longer has the power to fertilize the egg.

Will a vasectomy change the way you feel about sex? As in sterilization for women, you may have emotional responses to a vasectomy, which should be considered seriously. For some men the continuing possibility of fathering a child, even though they don't use it, is very important. This may be tied up with all sorts of ideas about virility and however rational a method vasectomy may seem, these feelings about yourself are important. If neglected, they may spill over into doubts about your ability to make love.

It is not uncommon to hear that difficulties have started 'after my vasectomy'. Of course, the episode of the vasectomy may well occur just as some of the pressures of the middle years begin to bite and it will provide an obvious peg to hang your problems on. So, again, this is something that needs to be honestly discussed by you both. You should not hold back from talking about uncomfortable subjects that seem unlikely to happen, such as: 'What would you feel if I died and you married again?' or 'What would happen if the unthinkable took place and we lost our children?'

Most surgeons will ask you these questions before they undertake a vasectomy, but it is useful to have thought them over quietly beforehand.

So which contraceptive should you use?

Perhaps what emerges again from our look at the possible methods is that it is important to find out the facts that pinpoint which kinds of contraception are suitable for either or both of you. This can mean a discussion with your community nurse or your family doctor, if they have time, or with the staff of your local family planning contraceptive clinic. They are specially trained to assess all methods and to find the ones appropriate to your needs.

Find something for your own situation
The changes that occur in the middle years will require special consideration. These will primarily affect the woman, since after the age of forty the Pill, even the mini-pill, will probably not be suitable and the irregularities of the menopause may militate against the IUD. It may be a time when the man has to take more responsibility for contraception, and he may well have anxieties about the sheath as well as vasectomy. Both partners may be sorry that the time of comparatively care-free contraception on the Pill is over and yet feel middle age is no time to risk additional pregnancies.

Taking all these facts and considerations into account, do discuss the alternatives with each other. Sometimes you may decide to share responsibility: she will use the cap at the mid-cycle and more fertile part of her cycle, he will use the sheath at other times; or she will use the mini-pill, but if it doesn't suit her he will consider a vasectomy. This discussion can also be a means of sharing anxieties about unwanted pregnancies and can sometimes help to explain and sort out some of the misunderstandings that have arisen between you over sex.

10   SOLO

Sexuality and sexual feelings are not the prerogative of those who are married or who have stable relationships. There are those who reach the middle years and are single, and men and women who are or will become widowed or divorced. As people on their own they will still have to deal with the sexual part of themselves.

The single person

By this I mean the person who has reached middle age and who has never had a fully sexual relationship with another person or at most has had only a temporary affair.

Men

Men are in a rather different position from women. They remain fertile most of their lives and, therefore, provided they marry a woman who is young enough they can always offer the possibility of children to the partner. Moreover, even in modern times in the Western world, it is often men who propose marriage and women who accept or turn down their proposal.

However, this doesn't alter the fact that the very reason why you have not proposed to any woman may be that you are shy and uncertain of your masculinity. It may equally, of course, have been circumstances of time and space or a vow of celibacy that have prevented a close relationship with a woman. In any case, men have differing ways of coping with their sexual needs. Some may be able, through training or preference, to suppress all physical expressions of sex; others find relief in masturbation or casual relationships. They are not immune, however, to all the pressures and stresses that are part of growing older and they may have to add to them a sense of loneliness. Many adjust and live their lives to the full, have plenty of friends and actually enjoy their bachelorhood, but many find it increasingly difficult and themselves more and more alienated, not only from women, but also from those whom they view as 'real men'.

Women

Women have different problems. There is the obvious watershed of the menopause (see Chapter 6), and getting married and having babies when you are over forty has its own difficulties. It can, however, be done. A colleague of mine married at forty and had her children at forty-two and forty-four, meanwhile carrying on most successfully with her career in a teaching hospital; neither pregnancy caused her any problems. But even in these days when single women have a much happier and more fulfilling role in society and some choose a career in preference to marriage, there are still many who would have liked a steady partner and family and have not had them because 'nobody asked me'.

Again, more women than men tend to be pulled in to look after their ageing parents and consequently feel that they must not and often do not have the chance to make close relationships which might lead to marriage.

Women have the same recourse as men to suppression of their sexual activity, masturbation and perhaps, to casual relationships.

Nothing to be ashamed about

Some of you who are single will have adapted more or less happily to your life; you may have all that you need for yourself, you may prefer to go solo. Others may have regrets and half-admitted longings. Whatever your situation, don't be afraid of your sexual feelings. I have known people who have resented and been bitterly ashamed of their sexual feelings about themselves and towards others that seem suddenly to have overwhelmed them – 'and at my age too!' Why not? We are sexual beings. Powerful sexual feelings may be much more difficult to cope with if you feel there is no way they can or ought to be expressed openly, although they are a part of you as a human being. Because they are not returned does not invalidate them or make you less of a sexual being.

Seek advice

Some of this anxiety about your own sexuality may arise when you do decide to get married for the first time in middle age. If you have any anxieties it is sensible to go and talk to your family doctor, telling him or her frankly of the situation. If you feel, as a woman, that it is difficult to talk openly before a male doctor, then family planning, or contraceptive, clinics are always ready to talk things over, even if having a family is no longer likely. In any case, it is sensible for a woman to have an examination, at least to make sure that she has not got a tight hymen or vaginismus (see pages 84 and 86). Also, for both men and women, even in these days of widespread sexual information, it is possible that you may have led the sort of life in which you haven't had a chance to explore fully the facts of sex. Better by far to check out what you know or don't know with someone who can deal sympathetically with your questions.

The widow or widower

To lose your partner is a shattering blow. If the loss takes place in the middle years, before you have reached old age together, it can bring many other problems besides your own grief. You may still be responsible for a growing family, and because of this you will have to take on the role of the other parent as well. This means that a man will have to think of home-making activities and a woman of earning at least some part of her income when she may not have worked for some time. Throughout, the one who is bereaved is deprived of the very support and comfort that would have helped in undertaking these added responsibilities. Part of that support and comfort will have been sexual activity, the holding close, the caressing, the valuing and the physical evidence of loving and giving. In one sudden moment all this is taken away, just when it is most needed.

A friend of mine, Dora, once told me that widowhood had further implications. Although her husband died quite suddenly, he had been ill on and off for several years and she knew that his death might occur at any time. Her children were grown up and had left home and they often visited her and were a great support, but she said what she longed for more than anything was 'a man's shoulder to lean on, a man's arm around me.' She said that she still loved her husband and didn't think she would want to marry again, but that this yearning for physical contact with a man was a real basic need.

She went on to explain further what had happened. She was a petite, pretty woman, very feminine, but also very tough underneath and competent. When her husband was alive they had a large number of friends and when they met, not only would the women embrace but their men friends and the husbands of these women would give Dora a hug and a kiss and she would often be swept along with an arm round her waist. Immediately after her husband's death all this stopped. Not only were her women friends less able to embrace her warmly – 'I think', she said, 'they are afraid that I might burst into tears' – but all physical contact from their husbands stopped. 'I seem to be surrounded by a sort of fence of my widowhood.'

Dora was a woman who was able to look with understanding at what was happening to herself and her friends She admitted freely that her husband had confirmed and reinforced her sexuality and that she needed this. She understood at least to some degree why her friends, especially the men, found it difficult to touch her, but it didn't ease the longing or the hurt that this withdrawal caused. Sometimes this kind of longing may make you feel that you are being disloyal to your partner. 'How could I be thinking of myself when he or she is so recently dead?' 'How can I want another man's arm around me, or another woman's soft touch?'

Be fair to yourself. If anything, this kind of longing is a tribute to all the good things you had from your partner and your love-making. It is a deep and intimate loss and perhaps the one that it is most difficult to speak about.

Odd one out

Socially, the loss of husband or wife is difficult too. On the whole the 'spare man' is better off than the 'spare woman' in society, though perhaps this is changing slightly. In any case, it is likely that at first invitations will not be so frequent and you may feel cut off from friends that you once saw quite often. People are afraid of death and they often do not know how to cope with their friends' bereavement.

If you are bereaved, it will take some time to come out from the effects of loss. Feel able to take your time, not to stay stagnant in the pool of sorrow, but nevertheless to recognize that the steps towards the shore may be slow and painful. Physical loss will come upon you suddenly, and often with intense mental anguish. No, you are not going mad – this is frequently part of the way back; though if, after a year, you still feel totally weighed down by grief, do seek professional help. You will climb out in the end and all that your partner meant to you will go with you and give you strength.

If you are a friend of the one who is going through this stage you should be able to understand what is happening and be the one to offer the kiss, to hold him or her close, to let them lean on you and to tell you their longings. You cannot replace the loved one, but you can offer physical evidence of your caring.

Starting again: new patterns of courtship

Of course, some people find new partners and marry again. There are many adjustments which have to be made when this occurs and one of them is on the physical level. Whether or not your new partner has been married before, you will have to explore each other's sexuality from the beginning again.

You may find it difficult to begin courting all over again and physical expressions of caring, especially in the early stages of learning to touch and to kiss again, and building your own private set of signals between each other may feel strange for you both at first, especially when you are not sure what reaction to expect. You may have growing or grown-up families and their presence may be unexpectedly embarrassing, especially as they sometimes resent someone whom they feel will usurp the position of their dead father or mother. Awareness of the problems that children of a former marriage can pose may make it more difficult to move towards a sexual relationship with each other.

In any case, this relationship will be different and, because your expectations and assumptions are based on previous experience, it will be inevitable that some comparisons will be made. Your partner may be aware of this too, and so it is even more important that you should be able to discuss freely your needs and likes and dislikes. What you build up as a sexual pattern between you will never be a carbon copy of what went before. It will have its own special delight if you can be honest with each other, and open to fresh ways of expressing sexual love.

Divorce

Divorce is becoming increasingly common in Britain: in 1982 one in five of all marriages ended in divorce, the incidence being highest in recently married young couples. Though it may sometimes be by mutual consent, it is seldom other than painful and demoralizing. If it occurs in middle age, and the home and family you have built together is now shattered, it can be profoundly traumatic for both partners. Even if one partner has now become involved with someone else, the whole process of untying the many links that bind you together is certain to be difficult and in many cases can be further embittered by legal wrangles about alimony and access, and what is to happen to the family home. One partner may have had to endure ill-treatment of one sort or another. Sometimes the loyalties of children are split and the parent they reject is caused extra pain. Sometimes if they are old enough, the children reject both parents.

Sex becomes a casualty
Inevitably at some point sexual relations have been affected. Sexual intercourse may have been infrequent and unsatisfactory. One partner may have wanted it, the other been cold. If someone else is involved and intercourse between the couple has been affected, the sense of rejection, of not being good enough or attractive enough is great. Sometimes the husband has maintained regular sex with his wife in spite of also having sex with the other woman. Often the wife will then feel 'I've been used', 'I feel dirty when I know he's been with her.' She may even feel that she has been blackmailed into agreeing to sex for fear of losing her husband altogether.

Some men, on hearing that their wife has had a lover, feel quite unable to compete and may become temporarily impotent (see Chapter 7).

When the traumas of the final split-up are added to all this, the woman is sometimes left with a total revulsion against sex and indeed a sense of betrayal that extends to her feelings about all men: 'That's what they're like. Use you, suck all they can get out of you, take none of the responsibility and then leave you.'

Similarly, men can feel that their masculinity has taken a severe knock and they are suspicious of women whom they feel dazzle and deceive them.

Picking up the pieces

After a divorce both partners have to rebuild their lives. They may be relieved to get out of the atmosphere of rows and constant bitterness, but they may be left very hurt and unsure of themselves. Even the partner who has left to make a new relationship may be dogged by regret and guilt.

This new relationship may not prove to be as good as it seemed to be. What was exciting and satisfying sex may not be so wonderful when it has to flourish on less money and someone else's demands to face up to. Your new partner may not find taking over part of your previous family as easy as you both hoped. You may find that some old friends are on your previous partner's side. There may even be the added complication of your new partner's earlier marriage and family. With these factors all leaving their mark, sexual relations may be quite difficult for a time. Often the new couple will feel rather desperately that this time it has to work. Comparisons with the past, however much you try to avoid them, may well arise in both your minds and you may begin to worry about how your partner's previous wife or husband rated in bed before things broke up.

The injured party

If this is so with those who wanted the break, how much more difficult it is for the ones who have been deserted. Their self-image may well be in ruins and they can be suspicious and angry with the opposite sex.

When a new relationship offers itself they may be wary and mistrustful. Often even if it develops on a basis of being friends, a tight restraint may be exercised on the sexual side, or at any rate on any real letting go in sex. You may find that you are able to let your new friend hold and kiss you in a superficial way, but that it is difficult to respond. When the relationship has become established each may feel that unless they make some sexual advances they may lose their new partner. Some even marry on the 'friends' basis, not having discussed the sexual side fully, only to find it difficult to let go altogether. This is perhaps more likely in the case of the woman, who will allow her new partner to have intercourse, but will not be able to respond in more than a passive way. She may unconsciously be protecting herself from a further let-down; she finds it difficult to give all for fear that she will once more be rejected.

The man may find it difficult to express real tenderness when this has previously been rejected. He, too, may be gripped by sexual need and achieve entry and ejaculation but find it difficult to ask for or to give gentle and relaxed expressions of love.

Don't let the pattern repeat itself

Do seek help if this sort of thing happens, otherwise the pattern may become fixed and unchanging and the hurt and insecurity be repeated. You may find some of the following points helpful in trying to readjust.

How to readjust to being on your own

In all the situations I have described in this chapter, there are certain processes that can help you to adjust.

1. Accept yourself as a valid sexual being. Allow yourself to have feelings about yourself and about the opposite sex and acknowledge these as right and proper.

You have needs as a sexual being that you can define to yourself, even though you may see that they are not likely to be fulfilled. There is nothing wrong in saying, 'I would like to be married and have children.' At the same time, you may well decide that in the present circumstances you are not likely to achieve this.

2. Decide what can be done about this as positively as you can. You may make up your mind to shrug your shoulders and concentrate on your garden. You may decide that you will at least put yourself in the way of making friends of your own sex. Or you may actively seek friends of the opposite sex. If you feel in control of yourself and happy with yourself, others will respond.

3. Give yourself time to recover from loss or rejection; and time to adjust to yourself afterwards.

4. Allow time for relationships to develop and time to make up your mind.

5. Don't look only at negative signs even though you may not be confident of your own sexuality.

6. When you establish a new sexual relationship be aware that it is a new event. Old hurts and wounds may not yet be fully healed and the scars will still be sensitive.

7. Do talk openly with your new partner – about your hopes and needs, about your anxieties, about what you like and don't like when you are making love.

8. Seek help from your family doctor, family planning (contraceptive) practitioner or counsellor if things seem not to be going well and you find you can't move forward as you would like.

11 ENJOY SEX IN THE MIDDLE YEARS

The middle years can be a wonderful part of your life. You have had your early struggles, you have met and fallen in love with each other, you have built a life together, often with a family that is now growing up and you may be having the pleasure of seeing them, in turn, find partners and start new families. Inevitably, in a book like this we have to look at the areas of stress and the difficulties that may arise, but I hope that in reading it you will have understood why some of these situations can affect your sexual life together and be able either to take avoiding action or positive steps to enhance your sex life.

Most of you probably accept that sex is an important part of marriage or of a stable relationship. It isn't necessarily the most important part, and couples vary in how, how much, and how often they express their care for each other through sex. Nobody has the right to tell a couple what they should or should not do to express sexual feelings between them, provided that neither is harming his or her partner or himself or herself, and provided that each is content and happy with the situation.

Sometimes, however, you will both feel that sex isn't as good as it used to be, or that there must be something more to it, or that what satisfies one of you neither satisfies nor actually pleases the other. Often, as you have discovered in this book, one partner has no idea that the other isn't happy, and it may be that the one who isn't really satisfied has never even been able to acknowledge this. This may be because a relationship is going through a difficult time, or it may be the cause of those difficulties, especially if other pressures are around at the same time.

It can simply be that your relationship has gone a little stale; it may be that there are profound and deep-seated problems between you. Sometimes there are physical difficulties which set up problems in sex which, if they are not discussed and understood, can cause friction between the two of you. You may blame your partner for something which he or she cannot help and then jump to the conclusion that you are no longer cared for. Perhaps the most difficult thing to realize is that because it is so tied up with the feelings you have for each other, and for yourselves, even slight changes in sexual behaviour can set up a whole series of repercussions within your relationship.

Some unattached people, it is true, see sex as a comparatively trivial matter, an expression of their own physical need that brings them pleasure and satisfaction and which they feel hurts no consenting partner. They are not concerned with permanent relationships and if one sexual encounter isn't as good as they hoped they can always find another. Perhaps they are for ever seeking for the perfect relationship which never comes their way.

Most people, in their hearts, long for a stable relationship with one other person that takes account of the needs of both. Both want to receive and to give love and care and are prepared to work for this ideal. Yes, there are break-ups, but most people would prefer to avoid them if they could. Sex can often be the focus for the difficulties that arise and even the few symptoms that stem from physical causes soon get overlaid with the painful feelings they provoke, so that in the end it is the relationship which suffers. Tension in the relationship itself often sets up sexual tension. So it is the relationship between you to which I as a counsellor constantly look for answers as to what has gone wrong, or to what has become stale and unsatisfactory.

To keep your relationship strong, you need to want things to remain as good as in the past, or to improve; preferably you will both want this. You will have to sort out what are simply the consequences of getting older, such as increased fatigue or lack of time, from what is preventable, such as being overtired and having no spare time at all. You can compensate for bodily changes and make sure that you keep fit and healthy; you can see that you eat sensibly, have enough sleep and exercise and balance work and recreation.

You may sometimes – and this is often difficult for very conscientious people – have to allow yourself and your partner to relax and take things more easily. An old and wise physician said to me in my younger, bustling days when I was getting too many nagging headaches 'There is no law against putting your feet up for half an hour after lunch.' I have reason to be very grateful to him, and I have come to see that this simple advice enables me to do more than before, with increased zest. Taking time off to have your hair done or to read a book can enable you to feel refreshed and relaxed in yourself and give you increased energy to cope with daily pressures. Above all, time off together to be open with each other, to listen to what each is saying, to cherish each other will do much to strengthen and renew your partnership and your own morale.

So, constantly you will come back to relationships. Even if you are now on your own, your appreciation of your own sexuality will depend on the quality of relationships in the past as well as in the present. If you have a steady relationship, you need to feel good in yourself and so does your partner; you need to do all that you can lovingly and positively to make each other feel good; you need to talk to each other and try to understand what your partner needs; you have to meet the challenge of change from whatever cause and adapt to each other's new needs if necessary; sometimes you may need help. This sensitive nurturing of your relationship will be the solid foundation for a full and satisfying sex life together.

WHOM YOU CAN TURN TO FOR HELP: USEFUL ADDRESSES

Do realize that a few simple questions asked early on, even a short discussion with someone who is sympathetic and knowledgeable, can help you through anxieties, and reactions to those anxieties, that might otherwise become more intense and turn a comparatively straightforward situation into a real problem. Here are some sources of help.

1. Family doctors.
2. Community nurses, or health visitors.
3. Family planning or contraceptive clinics.
4. Clinics specializing in sexual difficulties, usually attached to large hospitals; your doctor may refer you to one of these.
5. Marriage counsellors: the National Marriage Guidance Council in Britain has set up alongside its usual counselling service over forty clinics specializing in marital sexual therapy. There are also Catholic and Jewish organizations that give help to those of their faiths; and organizations for specific diseases such as diabetes or coronary heart disease can supply information about related sexual difficulties, as can Sexual Problems of the Disabled (SPOD: see Chapter 5).
   Addresses are listed below. For local branches, look in your telephone directory.

UNITED STATES

American Association of Marriage and Family Therapy
1717 K Street, NW, Suite 401
Washington, DC 20006

American Institute of Family Relations
5287 Sunset Boulevard
Los Angeles, California 90027

Association of Couples for Marriage Enrichment, Inc.
459 S Church Street
PO Box 10596
Winston-Salem, North Carolina 27108

Christian Home and Family Ministries
United Methodist Church
1908 Grand Avenue, Box 189
Nashville, Tennessee 37202

The Counselling and Psychotherapy Center
0–100 27th Street
Fair Lawn, New Jersey 07410

Family Service Association of America
44 East 23rd Street
New York, New York 10010

Masters and Johnson Institute
24 South Kingshighway
St Louis, Missouri 63108

National Institute of Marriage and Family Relations
6116 Rolling Road, Suite 316
Springfield, Virginia 22152

National Council on Family Relations
1219 University Avenue, SE
Minneapolis, Minnesota 55414

GREAT BRITAIN

The Association of Sex and Marital Therapists
(ASMT)
Whiteley Wood Clinic
Woofindin Road
Sheffield S10 3TL

Family Planning Association
27/35 Mortimer Street
London W1N 7RJ

International Planned Parenthood Association
18–20 Lower Regent Street
London SW1

The Institute of Marital Studies
Tavistock Centre
Belsize Lane
London NW3 5BA

National Marriage Guidance Council
Herbert Gray College
Little Church Street
Rugby CV21 3AP

Sexual Problems of the Disabled
The Diorama
14 Peto Place
London NW1

NORTHERN IRELAND

Armagh Marriage Advisory Centre
Oakleigh
Thomas Street
Portadown

Northern Ireland Family Planning Association
47 Botanic Avenue
Belfast BT7 1JL

Northern Ireland Marriage Guidance Council
76 Dublin Road
Belfast BT2 7HP

IRELAND

Irish Family Planning Association
15 Mountjoy Square
Dublin 1

Marriage Counselling Service
24 Grafton Street
Dublin

CANADA

The Canadian Association for Marriage and Family Therapy
271 Russell Hill Road
Toronto
Ontario M4V 2T5

Family Service
55 Parkdale Avenue
Ottawa
Ontario K1Y 4G1

Planned Parenthood Federation of Canada
151 Slater Street
Suite 200
Ottawa
Ontario K1P 5H3

The United Church House
85 St Clair Avenue East
Toronto 7
Ontario

AUSTRALIA

Australian Federation of Family Planning Associations
70 George Street
Sydney
New South Wales 2000

Marriage Divorce Counselling Centre
1 Ord Street
Perth 6000

Marriage, Reconciliation and Separation Counselling
262 Pitt Street
Sydney
New South Wales 2000

National Marriage Guidance Council of Australia
6 Morton Road
Burwood
Victoria 3125

NEW ZEALAND

National Marriage Guidance Council of New Zealand
PO Box 2728
Wellington

New Zealand Family Planning Association
PO Box 68200
Newton
Auckland 1

SOUTH AFRICA

Cape Town Marriage Guidance Council
309 Groote Kirk Building
Cape Town

Family Planning Association of South Africa
412 York House
46 Kerk Street
Johannesburg 2001

ACKNOWLEDGEMENTS

I would like to thank my patients and clients through the years for all that I have learnt in working with them.

I am very grateful to all members both medical and lay, of the Family Planning Clinics in which I work for their cheerful and enthusiastic co-operation and I would especially thank Sister Edna Ball, SRN for her skilful co-therapy.

To all my colleagues in the National Marriage Guidance Council I want to say how much I appreciated and enjoyed our shared explorations in the field of counselling; this book could not have been written without that experience. My thanks go especially to Bob Grafton, Manager of the NMGC bookshop, who first suggested the need for this book; and to Alison Clegg, Project Officer for NMGC's Marital Sexual Therapy, and her husband, Dr David Clegg, both of whom read the manuscript and made several helpful suggestions.

I would like to thank my daughter-in-law, Catherine Banting, for making sense of and typing my manuscript.

Finally I would like to thank Martin Dunitz, Piers Murray Hill and Mary Banks for guiding me, comparatively painlessly, from first draft to final book form.

1983   CHRISTINE E. SANDFORD

The publishers are grateful to the following individuals and organizations for their help in the preparation of this book:

For permission to reproduce photographs: Art Directors Photo Library (page 52); Colour Library International (page 42); and Zefa Picture Library (pages 49 and 80).

The cover photograph was taken by Jan Kuczerawy and the location photographs by Dave Brown. The modelling was done by Penny Rigden and Steve Rome. The bedwear was kindly lent by Dorma, Manchester.

The diagrams were drawn by Cathy Clench.

INDEX

Figures in *italics* refer to illustrations

Other books in the Positive Health Guide series

ANXIETY AND DEPRESSION
A practical guide to recovery
Prof Robert Priest

We all get anxious and depressed at times, but for at least one person in ten these feelings are so overwhelming that they totally disrupt their lives. Prof Priest explains exactly what anxiety and depression are, what causes them, and what you can do to speed your own recovery – including relaxation and massage, ways of coping with difficult relationships,and when to seek medical advice.

STRESS AND RELAXATION
Self-help ways to cope with stress and relieve nervous tension, ulcers, insomnia, migraine and high blood pressure
Jane Madders

Jane Madders has developed her own simple technique of natural relaxation that will help to reduce stress in your everyday life. Tension headaches, migraine, insomnia and even nervous breakdown can often be relieved by learning to relax.

HIGH BLOOD PRESSURE
What it means for you, and how to control it
Dr Eoin O'Brien and Prof Kevin O'Malley

Written by two eminent physicians, this comprehensive and practical guide to detecting, preventing and controlling high blood pressure gives suggestions on how to measure your own pressure, take daily exercise and control your diet; and up-to-date information on the drugs in use today.